D1175034

Parenting Your Superstar

How to help your child get the most out of sports

Parenting Your Superstar

How to help your child get the most out of sports

Robert J. Rotella, PhD
University of Virginia
Linda K. Bunker, PhD
University of Virginia

Leisure Press
Champaign, Illinois

Library of Congress Cataloging-in-Publication Data

Rotella, Robert J.
  Parenting your superstar.

  Bibliography: p.
  Includes index.
  1. Sports for children.   2. Parent and child.
I. Bunker, Linda K.   II. Title.
GV709.2.R6   1987   796'.01'922   84-20174
ISBN 0-88011-262-X

Developmental Editor: Patricia Sammann
Production Director: Ernie Noa
Copy Editor: John Beck
Typesetter: Sandra Meier
Text Layout: The Admakers
Cover Photograph: Photo by Kirk Schlea/Berg & Associates
Cover Design and Layout: Scott Reuman
Interior Photographs: Photo on page xviii is from C.J. Mullins
  (1983). *A parent's guide to youth soccer.* New York: Leisure
  Press, p. x. Photo on page 91 is from G.B. Dintiman (1984). *How
  to run faster.* New York: Leisure Press, p. 38.

ISBN: 0-88011-262-X

Printed in the United States of America

10   9   8   7   6   5   4   3   2   1

Leisure Press
A division of Human Kinetics
Box 5076   Champaign, IL 61820
1-800-DIAL-HKP
1-800-334-3665 (in Illinois)

This book is dedicated to our parents, Tony and Billie Bunker and Guido and Laura Rotella, whose love and pride in us helped us to believe in ourselves. Their wisdom and guidance led us to appreciate the joys and happiness that sport participation can bring. It is also dedicated to our extended family of brothers and sisters, aunts, uncles, grandparents, and cousins who supported and challenged us to be the best that we could be; to daughter Casey Rotella, our nieces and nephews, the children with whom we have worked, and particularly to Gabriella Casero, John Short, Kandi Kessler, and Pat Hunter; and to all the young athletes at the Eastside Swim and Racquet Club and the Brandon Training School, and in the Youth Sport programs of Charlottesville-Albemarle County, North Carolina, and Homewood-Flossmoor, Illinois.

Acknowledgments

We gratefully acknowledge the support and encouragement of Darlene Rotella and Diane Wakat. Their patience and insights contributed immeasurably to our freedom to write and our understanding of various aspects of child rearing and sport.

We also express our appreciation to Nina Seaman for her secretarial assistance and her perceptive editorial and "parental" suggestions. We would also like to thank John and Terry Billing, Butch and Angela Paul, David and Linda Ojala, Bruce and Barbara Chaloux, Nick and Flor Tomassetti, Davis Love, Sarah Odom, and DeDe Owens for their advice on this manuscript.

Golf Digest magazine. From January 1982 issue. Copyright ©
1982.

p. 70-71, Adapted from "He Comes in Second" by R.H. Coulson
Swimmers Magazine, December 1978, p. 12. Copyright 1978 by
Swimmers Magazine. Adapted by permission.

p. 72, From "The Real Meaning of Winning" by B. Close, *Swimmers
Magazine*, December 1978, p. 12. Copyright 1978 by *Swimmers
Magazine*. Reprinted by permission.

p. 82-83, From "Do's and Don'ts for Self-Confidence" by C. Fisher.
Paper presented at the annual Sport Psychology Conference,
Charlottesville, VA, June 1982. Reprinted by permission.

p. 102, Excerpted from "Finding the Right Teacher for Your Child"
by Davis Love. Permission Golf Digest magazine. From January
1982 issue. Copyright © 1982.

p. 107, The following is reprinted courtesy of SPORTS ILLUS-
TRATED from the December 14, 1981 issue. Copyright © 1981
Time Inc. "Catch a Catching Star" by John Underwood. ALL
RIGHTS RESERVED.

p. 132, The following is reprinted courtesy of SPORT ILLUS-
TRATED from the August 17, 1981 issue. Copyright © 1981 Time
Inc. "Love and Hate in El Segundo" by John Garrity. ALL RIGHTS
RESERVED.

p. 134-135, From "Can the Caulkins Sisters Survive Success?" by
T. Power, *Swimmers Magazine*, June-July 1980, p. 6. Copyright
1980 by *Swimmers Magazine*. Reprinted by permission.

p. 137-138, From "Inside Track" by D. Schultz, *Inside Sports*,
December 11, 1981. Copyright 1981 by *Inside Sports*. Reprinted
by permission.

p. 139, The following is reprinted courtesy of SPORTS ILLUS-
TRATED from the December 15, 1980 issue. Copyright © 1980
Time Inc. "The Master of Disaster" by Bruce Newman. ALL
RIGHTS RESERVED.

p. 139, 140, Excerpted from "Tips to Parents of Junior Players"
by Nancy Lopez. Permission Golf Digest and Nancy Lopez. From
May 1981 issue. Copyright © 1981.

p. 211, From *The Struggle That Must Be* (pp. 237-238) by H.
Edwards, 1980, New York: Macmillan. Copyright 1980 by H.
Edwards. Reprinted by permission.

p. 224, From *The Teenage Survival Book* (p. 81) by S. Gordon,
1981, New York: Times Books, a Division of Random House, Inc.
Copyright 1981 by Times Books. Reprinted by permission.

Contents

Preface

As authors, we cannot help but reflect upon the experiences that our parents provided for us when we were children. Our parents loved us very much and appreciated the potential of sport for helping us to grow and mature in a happy and healthy way. They were not highly trained physical educators, coaches, or teachers, but their wisdom was clear in everything they did.

We remember the days when our parents returned home after a tiring day of work only to be greeted by our request for a game of catch or to "shoot some hoops." They were usually happy to play. They seldom said "I'm too tired," never seemed to complain, and always seemed to look for opportunities to hug us and let us know that they were proud of us.

We remember those first days of organized sport—our tear-filled eyes after failure and our bright smiles after success. We wanted so much to please our parents, but we knew that whether we won or lost, played well or didn't play at all, our parents would be there to console us or to congratulate us. Often they patiently listened to us replay our successes over and over. Whenever we questioned our ability, Mom or Dad was there to encourage and support us.

Today, 20 million children participate in organized sport. The United States has the most extensive amateur sports program in the world. Coaches and officials generally volunteer their services. Parents search for sport programs in which their children can participate, and children crave opportunities to play. Together, we can all help to make the sport experience positive for the children of today and tomorrow.

Adults, particularly parents, play a crucial role in the success and happiness of children in sport. The information presented in this book has been useful to many young athletes. We are excited about the possibility that this knowledge will be useful to many parents and children who share our appreciation for the joy and value of sport.

Youth sport is rapidly expanding and evolving into a highly organized and challenging endeavor. The time and energy that must be committed have expanded greatly. More and more young athletes are taking sport seriously at an early age. As a result of these factors, problems have arisen that have the potential for eroding many of the benefits of early sport experiences, and the parents' role has become even more crucial. This book is intended to help parents to be as effective as possible in guiding their highly committed children toward joyful and successful experiences in sport.

Introduction

Parents of children who make a serious commitment to sport face a difficult challenge: to raise a happy, healthy, and successful child. It is not a responsibility that can be taken lightly, and certainly not a simple one. Parents and society place special importance on children's involvement in sport because of the positive qualities such as sportsmanship, teamwork, self-confidence, and skill development that athletics can teach. How can you as parents help provide a sport experience that will be positive, enjoyable, and successful?

There are no simple or magical answers. When it comes to raising a child, there are no absolute rights or wrongs. No one is an expert in every aspect of parenting; no one should expect to be. Love, concern, pride, and emotional support aren't displayed according to a mathematical formula, nor does mixing them together ensure a perfect solution. Parenting is an art, not a science; parents must provide a unique mixture for each child. You know your child better than anyone else, and you can draw upon information in this book to make athletics a positive and special experience for your child.

The sport world today seems to demand that your child mature at an early age. You need to be concerned that your child may be robbed of the experience of growing up. Some adults do try to take the youthful fun out of sport. But you must also realize that in today's high-powered, specialized world your child may need to start in a specific sport at an early age if he or she ever wants to play competitively, especially at high levels of skill.

Undoubtedly your child will experience both excitement and discouragement once a commitment is made to an endeavor as challenging, publicly evaluated, and recognized as sport. Your child will need your help, love, and support throughout.

This book emphasizes that parents play a significant role in developing a child's interest and potential for success in sport. This means that you must make a commitment to your child's sports development. However, you must be realistic. You can't always be available to cater to your child and shouldn't want to be! But you can make the most of the time you spend together.

You must determine your priorities. The emphasis on the parents' role in this book is not intended to pressure you but rather to make you aware that you will influence your child's interest, level of commitment, and ultimate success in sport. The way you influence your child will greatly determine whether sport is a positive, growth-oriented experience that contributes to your child's health, happiness, and success.

You must not measure your effectiveness by your child's success in sport. You can do everything within your power and still not have a child who is a winning athlete. Some parents will do nothing and their child will still become a star. You must have as your goal providing your child with the *chance* to become the best he or she can be.

As you read this book, feel good about your possibilities as parents of a budding athlete. Don't allow yourselves to get lost in worry or guilt. If negative feelings do occasionally cross your minds, calmly sit back and ask yourselves if there is a reason for your guilt or worry. If not, forget it; if there is a reason, decide what you can do to eliminate the cause of the negative thoughts.

This book is intended to help the parents of the child who wishes to be a successful athlete in high-level competition. It is divided into three sections. Section I, Raising Your Child To Be an Athlete, will cover the parents' role in their child's participation in sport. Included will be information concerning your role, what it is like to be a parent of an athlete, choosing the best sport experiences, deciding when to start serious practices, and helping your child to reach competitive success. Section II, Guiding Your Child's Sport Experience, details how you can work with coaches and learn to deal with problems that arise in teaching your own child. Section II also includes basic information on how to teach, prevent injuries, and provide for the nutritional needs of a child athlete. Section III, Sport as a Total Experience, discusses the relationship between sport and competition, academic pressures and potential for athletic success, and the role of sport in developing the individual's skill in setting and meeting fulfilling goals.

Remember this book is not designed to teach you how to be the perfect parent for a child athlete. Rather it is intended to provide the best information available to help you create your own "recipe" for raising a happy and successful child athlete. Like any good recipe, it must be able to be expanded, changed, or modified to meet each situation. This book cannot make decisions for you or guarantee you or your child success and happiness. But it can help you to make choices that will increase the likelihood of your child's developing into a happy and successful athlete. We can provide the basics, we can discuss crucial issues, but *you* must follow the recipe and add the spice and tender loving care.

Section I

Raising Your Child
To Be an Athlete

Section I provides important information on whether athletes are born or made, how you can influence the development of skill, and how you affect the attitudes that your child develops toward competition and sport participation.

An important part of raising a happy child athlete is understanding your own values. How important do you think it is for your child to participate in sport? Is it important to you for your daughter or son to be highly successful? Do you believe social or academic success is related to sport participation? How much are you willing to "give" so your child can be successful in sport?

Understanding the implications of serious sport participation is essential to making good decisions. What will happen to your life as a parent if your child becomes a serious athlete? Special demands will be placed on you and your family in terms of time, money, and stress, but these demands can be handled in ways that can make your family stronger and happier.

The choice of one sport or several sports is a thorny issue. Should your child specialize at an early age, or should he or she be more well rounded? Which sport should be played: team or individual, popular or less popular, one in which the whole family can participate or one that the child can play best? And how will intense involvement in sport at an early age affect the child's relationships with other children?

Getting your child started right in sports is important to his or her future. You will need to help your child learn to set and achieve goals effectively. You also must wait until your child is ready for serious commitment to sport because different children will be ready at different times, depending on their physical and emotional maturity.

Finally, one of the biggest advantages your child can gain from sport is the ability to compete. You can teach your child to be a strong competitor in several ways: by showing the child the process of effective competition, by helping the child develop a competitive attitude, by instilling self-confidence in the child, by teaching the child self-discipline and time management skills, and by emphasizing the importance of fair play and positive values.

Your Role as Parents of an Athlete

Chapter 1

It has finally happened—your own youngster is a potentially fine athlete. You are glad your child is seriously interested in sport, but you also want your child to be happy. Although you hope the sport experience will lead your child to be happy, respected, confident, and well liked, you realize that even for young athletes sport can be highly competitive and at times frustrating and discouraging. In this chapter we discuss some typical challenges to parents and techniques and other actions that can make successful parenting in this situation more likely.

Unlike some parents, you are not overly ego-involved. You want to do what is best for your child, and you are well aware that sport has been a great experience for some children, but a problem for others. However, you would like your child to enjoy the benefits of sport, and you may even believe that a few disappointments would be good for your child's development. In the long run you know that your child will learn from these setbacks, and you would like him or her to enjoy meeting challenges and overcoming obstacles. Such an attitude will be helpful throughout life. That much you know for sure!

Interesting Your Child in Sport

For years, parents and scholars have debated whether athletes are "born" or "made." Today we know that successful athletes are both born *and* made! Many children inherit great natural ability and mature physically at an early age but never become successful. Other children inherit average physical talent but develop their mental and physical skills to excel in sport.

Parents undoubtedly play a crucial role in guiding their child's interest. Dan Marino, quarterback for the Miami Dolphins, said in an interview for *Inside Sports* (Whicker, 1982):

> The biggest thing in my early development is that my dad had a job where he could be home in the afternoon, waiting for me to get out of school. Then we would throw to each other the rest of the day. My dad keeps me in perspective. Plus he's the best coach I ever had. (p. 56)

With the increased pressure and rewards available to athletes, parents must understand how they can contribute to raising a child who is not only successful but *happy*. As a parent, if you can accomplish this task you can consider yourself successful and will probably become happier and more satisfied yourself. In the following sections, suggestions are presented on how you can foster a love of sport in your child.

Positive Parenting

Parents seem to find themselves constantly open to criticism: "Those parents sure messed up that kid"; "They tried to live through their child"; "That child sure is spoiled. His parents loved him so much they were afraid to discipline him." We hear far less talk about successful parents. When was the last time you heard someone say, "They're great parents. They did a lot of things right for their child"? Or, "Gosh, those parents are so patient. Their child was failing at everything for years, and they were always so encouraging." Or, "Wow! I don't know how he does it. That father stands on his feet and works hard all day, yet he always has energy to play with his children after work." Or, "That mother is amazing. Her husband left her when their child was very young, and yet the daughter has become an excellent athlete. She helped a lot." Perhaps you haven't heard too much praise of this sort. But parents such as these have done admirable jobs of raising their children.

In this book we explore the behaviors and strategies of positive parenting. Raising a child who can participate happily and successfully in sport will indeed be a challenge. Attaining success in sport is difficult, and some failure is inevitable for every sport participant. Moments of great joy as well as moments of frustration and disappointment are certain. Combining success with happiness is twice as hard.

How well you guide your child through these experiences will be crucial. Success will require you to develop a *close, trusting relationship* with your child. This is the first step, one that all effective parents, coaches, and teachers must take. You must be able to build a caring and warm relationship with your child that is constant and consistent. From this base of trust, you and your child will be free to talk openly. In this way you will better understand your child and be able to provide the encouragement and support he or she needs.

Providing a Sport Role Model

Probably the most important thing that you can do to interest your child in sport is to participate actively in sports yourself. Children who see their parents engaging in sport use them as role models. This is especially true when parents emphasize the fun, enjoyment, and excitement of sport. Parents who participate in sport themselves will "pull their child along" by setting good examples rather than "pushing" by force or coercion.

Enjoying sport is much more important to children than their parents' level of skill or ability to perform. Children less than 6 or 7 years old will realize your skill level, or lack of it, only if you feel self-conscious and continually comment on how uncoordinated you are. Just play and have fun. Show your children that you accept yourself as you are and that you will accept them no matter what level of skill they achieve.

The importance of participation and adult involvement cannot be overemphasized. For young children, you can serve as an example of someone who enjoys participating and testing skill through competition and also as a role model for skills. As your child matures and becomes more skilled, your ability to perform will be known—your enjoyment is the important aspect. Do not try to overstate your skill, but be sure to discuss and display how much you believe in the value of competition and participation.

Children will be attracted to activities that appear to capture the interest and enthusiasm of their parents. Often they will imitate their parents, and they may soon show an interest in playing their parents' game. You should enthusiastically encourage children to play when you see that they want to participate. At this point, you can encourage motivation by placing your child's interest and enjoyment ahead of your own. Be sure that your child's early experiences with sport are filled with fun and happiness. A display of affection and pleasure directed both toward sport and toward your child is definitely beneficial at this time. *Be sure to emphasize that you love your child regardless of how successfully he or she plays.*

Expressing Genuine Interest in Your Child

Nothing makes children feel more important than to have someone show a genuine interest in them. When you talk with your young athlete, show a genuine interest. Ask about his or her favorite sport: "Did you have fun?" "Did you have a good practice?" Simply ask a general question that lets your child know you are interested and ready to listen. Listen attentively when your youngster starts talking. Offer encouragement and support when pertinent. *When asked, provide advice.*

You can show your genuine interest through the careful use of compliments. A newspaper columnist once suggested that every family should have a "compliment club" in which each person would be expected to compliment at least one other family member each day. Anyone who did not provide at least one positive statement about someone else was expected to place 25¢ in the "compliment kitty" that evening. A great idea for most families!

The importance of sincere compliments within a family cannot be overstated. Children feel good about themselves when their attention is focused on things they do well. A key to confidence is the ability to accept compliments and say thank you to the sender. This is a good lesson to learn early in life.

The art of complimenting a youngster becomes particularly valuable when you can point out progress made on some insecurity or weakness. For example, if a young soccer player has had a particularly hard time heading the ball, try to find something good to say about today's attempts. The child may then be able to relax and enjoy playing, which is likely to lead to a self-fulfilling prophecy: If you think you can, you will!

Many other tricks can be used in the "compliment game." For example, if you know your child is disappointed in a performance, you might say, "Your form looked great" or "You really hustled and gave it your best effort. I'm really proud of what a tough competitor you are!" Being complimentary and helping to provide realistic feedback or goals (chapter 4) are both very important.

The encouragement that parents provide and the pleasure that they openly show are key elements in how children feel about themselves and their sport. Focus on being positive; everyone enjoys being around happy and positive individuals. If parents can help their children learn to enjoy sport and see the good things in different situations, the youngsters will learn to see the good things in themselves and their competitors. Don't criticize or belittle your child's competitors; instead, point out their positive qualities as well as your child's positive qualities.

Deciding to Commit to Sport Early

Your child can benefit from an early entrance into sport. Because many children make an early commitment to sport, waiting even until age 12 or 13 may hurt a youngster's chance of playing on a high school team. But some kids are simply not ready to make a commitment to a sport before their teenage years. Undue pressure on some youngsters produces either increased resistance or problems much greater than a lack of interest in sport. Encourage your child, provide positive examples, and, most importantly, be honest about your feelings and your willingness to support your child's choices and commitments.

Two parents recently described their struggle to get their disinterested child involved in sport without being pushy. They decided to give the child a football for Christmas "from Santa." Their plan backfired. Their son opened the gift, looked up, and said, "Look, a football. I guess even Santa makes mistakes!"

Another recent case provides a good example of parents who were not willing to put forth the necessary effort for a child who showed an early interest in sport. A young mother told us that she wanted her daughter to become a figure skater and asked, "How do I get my child to like skating? I took her once and she was a little frustrated at her lack of success, but by the end of the day she was enjoying it." We encouraged the mother to take the child skating for several consecutive days so she could learn and improve. "Let the child enjoy seeing herself progress," we suggested. "Make sure the child enjoys herself. Get out and skate with her. Fall down with her and laugh and get back up. Praise her for trying and persisting. When she seems discouraged, explain to her that even Dorothy Hamill, the Olympic star, fell down often when she was starting to learn to skate." The mother's response to these suggestions was confused and negative: "But I don't want to take my child skating very often. It could become a real burden. Soon she'll want to go all the time. I'd rather not get into that. I have things that *I* like to do. On weekends I'd rather rest."

Parents must make decisions about what is important and set priorities. How important should sport be to your child's life? Which comes first: your interests or your child's? How will these needs be balanced?

A similar situation occurs with parents who are active in a lifetime sport such as golf or tennis. They often do not have the patience to spend time and energy playing with a child who lacks skill, preferring to play with friends who are equally skilled. They feel that they deserve this free time for their own pleasure. Every time their child expresses interest in playing, the child is rejected; then later they wonder why the child doesn't enjoy their sport.

You must realize that the more time you devote to playing your sport with your child early in the child's sport career, the easier it will be later. You may have to spend time and energy playing with your child during the developmental years, but doing so will increase your joy in playing together later, when his or her skill level has advanced. Remember, an early decision can be very important, but only if the child is *ready* and *willing* and only if parents happily accept the required demands.

Making Value Decisions

You may be uncertain about how to provide the right experiences for your child. This is *your* child, and you want to do what is best. But making decisions is difficult. Should you aspire to raise your child to be a champion? Or should you hope that your child will be a well-rounded student athlete who will participate in sport throughout life? Perhaps these goals are not mutually exclusive.

Committing to Your Values

Everyone you know seems to have an opinion about children and sport. Some of your closest friends think trying to raise a champion would be dangerous for your child. After all, the child who doesn't make it could end up frustrated forever. Others argue that "going for it" and striving to be the best are what every child should be taught. They feel that sport provides the ideal conditions to prepare children for the realities of adult life. Others believe that sport is simply for fun, nothing more and nothing less.

As you consider these viewpoints, you can become confused about what is best for your child. But regardless of your choice, your child will be influenced by it. All parents have values that they impart to their children either knowingly or unknowingly starting at birth. Parents typically teach their children to value what they themselves value. Some parents value academic work; some place emphasis on athletics; some stress both. Others feel that making money is the highest priority. Many parents teach their children the importance of having friends. Still others combine these values and emphasize a blend of attitudes.

Your child will establish an identity based largely on what you value. Your child will even learn to defend your family's values by observing you because not everyone will agree with your values. Have you and your friends ever criticized some local family because their lives seemed to revolve entirely around their young athlete? You argued that such single-minded dedication was crazy, and that the child would certainly end up unhappy. But the athlete's family viewed the situation quite differently. They talked with each other about the dedication and maturity their child developed, about how much closer sport made their family, or about how other kids were out wasting their time.

Parents who are certain about their values learn to defend their point of view. Children who communicate openly with their parents may quickly become committed to these values. Don't expect others to agree with your approach. Weigh the options, make a decision, and believe in it.

Some people might view such an approach as narrow-minded. It may be! But it provides a solid base from which to build. These parents are confident they are teaching the preferred values. Others, typically those who are less certain about their own values, feel children should be left to develop their own values as they grow. Often they are so concerned about not pushing their children that they fail to provide any direction at all. The result is children who are unable to deal with peer pressure. They never make their own decisions.

You must decide what you value as a parent. A child who speaks against your values may not be merely looking for direction but may have heard a peer or a teacher speak out against the values you have espoused. How do you respond? Do you speak with confidence? Do you explain and justify your values? Do you tell the child how and why others might feel differently?

If you don't respond, you should not be surprised if your child does not adopt your values. If you strongly believe that a particular sport is best for your child, then you must commit yourself to encouraging your child and providing opportunities to play at an early age. If you don't, expect your child to make the decision without you, but don't be upset or surprised if you disagree with your child's choice. Similarly, don't be surprised when the child rebels during the teenage years if you push too hard.

Be sure that your child understands the reasons behind family values. Encourage questioning of values and allow your child the freedom to inquire about differing viewpoints. Help your child to learn to live according to chosen values while respecting the values of others.

Choosing Priorities

As you probably have noticed, two very different sport value systems have been presented: specialization in one sport versus all-around participation in sports. Both have their strengths and weaknesses; both have their risks. Today's sport world appears to demand a very early commitment to a particular sport for an athlete to become a champion. But you do not have to encourage this specialization if your values favor the all-around athlete rather than the champion.

In other countries, specialization with balance is often considered the key to success. The tennis development program in Czechoslovakia is a good example. Their program has produced Martina Navratilova, Ivan Lendl, Hana Mandlikova, and Tomas Smid, all of whom are top professional tennis players. Most actively took part in some other sport such as soccer but specialized in tennis. Most Olympic and professional athletes in soccer, golf, volleyball, football, basketball, and baseball in the United States also participated in another sport while concentrating on one specific sport.

Early specialization does have its risks. Your child's dedication may lead to discouragement and "burnout." But children who "go for it" and don't become the best know that they had a chance and did their best. They learned a *process* of self-improvement that will be useful throughout their lives and took steps toward self-acceptance.

To have never tried is a different kind of risk. It is often a comfortable risk. Your child will always have an excuse and can always dream about what might have been. But in later life your child may blame you for failing to provide direction. By the time your child decides what to do, it may be too late. As parents you must decide which risks are best for your child.

If you decide that your child's becoming a champion is worth striving for, and if your child shares your interest, then commit yourselves to it. If fun and well-rounded sport involvement are your mutual goals, then commit yourselves to that. Like it or not, today's world demands that children decide upon their values early in life. If happiness and success are desired, guidance and direction will be needed.

Recently a young boy and his parents came to us for help. Billy wished to try out for the school soccer team, solo for the next school musical concert, and be the Junior Assistant Scout Master for his Boy Scout troop. Billy found it impossible to make up his mind so he did nothing and wasted months lamenting his inability to decide upon a direction.

Many people face this kind of situation because there are so many opportunities. Probably the most logical way to choose would be to try all options for an extended time before deciding. But today, delaying a decision may close off an option. Parents must help their children set priorities so they will be able to order their goals. Encourage your child to write the activity options available on separate pieces of paper. Then have the child list "pros" and "cons" for each in separate columns. After careful study of the lists, the child should make a decision. You can give your opinion, but you should let your child decide.

You and your child must remain flexible. Values and goals may slowly alter over the years, but constant goal changing may only ensure failure. The best way to prevent such vacillation is careful decision making. Remember, the world changes rapidly. To move ahead, you must have clearly defined values and goals.

Many changes will be required of you as you support your child's involvement in sport. You must understand the issues and be actively involved in the difficult and important decisions affecting your child's participation.

Champions' Advice to Parents

All-American athletes, although not experts on child-rearing, can provide valuable insights for parents. Their thoughts are particularly useful for parents of precocious or talented athletes. How should parents treat their children? Do parents play a role in their children's success in sport? If so, what is their role?

A female All-American cross-country champion talked with us about her parents:

Parents play a crucial role in sport success. My parents never pressured me to win or practice. They always seemed to be satisfied with my performance as long as I was enjoying athletics. Whenever I was frustrated or discouraged with my performance, my parents were always available with a positive and encouraging attitude. They never tried to coach me when I was having trouble. Actually, the lack of pressure from my parents probably made me more determined to do well. If I had believed that they were interested only in my winning every race, I would have become rebellious and given up the sport.

Parents who have a child who appears to be gifted should certainly encourage interest in sport. However, parents should also emphasize other areas of interest in addition to sport. Then if a child becomes disinterested in sport, she will not be limited and lost. Later, as a sport career develops, parents should always be ready to support their child's interests, even if outside of athletics.

Parents should not have to prompt their child to go to practice. Parents should listen and provide advice but always let their child make decisions to encourage self-reliance. Now that I am away from my parents at the university, I feel I have direction because I have always been allowed to decide for myself which avenue of interest I wanted to pursue. I am happy with myself and with the thought that my parents will always support my choices.

Another female All-American track athlete shared the following observations with us:

Since I have remained in track for several years, I have had the opportunity to see other athletes come and go. I have noticed that some parents constantly nagged the coach about their child. They were concerned about potential, success, and being number one rather than considering whether their child was happy. I recall one parent who was so intense about his son's running that he would badger his son to stay up front during workouts that were supposed to be low key. He interfered with the coach, wanting to know what his son's times were and if his son should be running faster. Needless to say, to this father's consternation, the son no longer runs.

Such observations are made in almost all sports. For example, an All-American quarterback in football offered the following suggestions as we talked with him:

> My parents always took considerable interest in my athletic progress. They were a constant source of encouragement by providing much needed enthusiasm and advice, especially during the low point of my athletic career. My mother undertook many essential tasks, such as uniform washing, transporting me to practice and games, and providing immediate support on the trip home. My father usually provided guidance. Whenever I suffered a setback or encountered a difficult situation, my father would be there to put everything into perspective. He had an uncanny ability to find a ray of hope in even the most difficult situations. Perhaps most importantly, he insisted that I strive for excellence both as a person and as an athlete. It was never enough to be good in only athletics or academics; excellence should be strived for in both areas.

Not all parent involvement is beneficial. A female athlete who had potentially Olympic-level skill in horse-showing commented to us on how a parent's involvement in a child's sport can be detrimental.

> I started riding when I was two. My mother always told me that I begged her to let me, but I was too young to remember. Anyway, at five I began showing ponies for other people. I was considered very good, and at age seven I had developed Olympic aspirations. But I'm not sure I ever enjoyed riding. I feel my mother's intense involvement with my career—she was my coach, my groom, and my financier—put such pressure on my competition that riding became unbearably frustrating. When I won, she reveled in my glory; when I lost, she made me feel that I had failed; when I didn't feel like working out, I didn't meet her standards of discipline and desire to achieve. In short, almost everything I did, I saw in my mother's terms, and very little of what I did was for me. At the time, however, it was hard for me to realize this, and even harder for me to call it quits. Even though I finally did quit, it was a gradual process. I sold my favorite pony when I was 14, and my heart was never in it after that. However, I held on apathetically for two more years until another sport gradually took over the central place in my life.

These examples reflect the important role that parents play in their children's sport success. Support and encouragement from home are essential even for gifted athletes. Many important concepts can be gained from the actions of parents of successful athletes. The key points suggested by All-Americans with whom we have worked include the following:

- Avoid pressuring a child about winning or losing.
- Do not force a child to practice.
- Emphasize enjoyment.
- Provide encouragement and hopeful optimism when needed.
- Encourage nonsport interests.
- Encourage self-reliance and acceptance of responsibility for decisions.
- Do not interfere with your child's coach.
- Help your child to develop and maintain a healthy perspective.
- Encourage your child to play for himself or herself—not for you or anyone else.
- Allow your child to set his or her own standards of excellence.
- Separate sport failure from personal failure.

What Sport Can Mean to Your Child

When you think of your child as being athletic, do you think in terms of a champion? Perhaps too often the champion image is the only image, but many of the happiest and healthiest athletes simply love playing and competing. They have never been the best, but they still enjoy trying to improve their performance. They have accepted themselves and their limitations. They like who they are. They also are healthy because they remain active in sport well into old age.

One 76-year-old super senior tennis champion recalled for us how his parents raised him:

My parents always had to work long, hard hours. But whenever they could, they would play some game with me—not necessarily tennis. Playing was always fun. I knew they loved it when I played because about the only reason I was ever excused from certain household chores was if I were playing a game.

After a game, table conversation always seemed to be dominated by talk of playing some game. Sometimes we would talk about failures and frustrations. Other times we just talked about other athletes that we admired. We didn't just talk about young kids; often we talked about older adults. So even early in life, emphasis was placed on three things: playing games with local kids so we could meet and make friends; playing at least one activity we could play for our entire life; and talking about positive things or about other people, or not talking at all.

Sport obviously means different things to different people. Your child will likely get out of sport whatever he or she aims to get from the experience. The most valuable experiences in sport seldom have much to do with putting a ball through a basket, hitting a ball over a fence or into a goal, walking on a balance beam, kicking a ball through goal posts, or crossing a line faster than others. Because the outside world emphasizes results, parents must help their child to gain the most important benefits from sport by emphasizing the following:

- Healthy exercise
- Learning to compete
- Patience and persistence
- Lifelong friendships
- Learning to lead and follow
- Dealing with winning or losing
- Developing emotional control
- Cooperation
- Respect for rules
- Satisfaction in doing one's best
- Positive thinking and optimism
- Lifelong activities

Be sure that you help your child to realize that there is more meaning to sport than winning or losing. If sport means nothing but winning or losing, sport probably isn't worth very much to your child.

Prepared Parenting

Raising a child is a most important responsibility, and raising a happy sport participant is even more challenging. Parents must realize that they have a great influence on the development of their child. Don't be upset if you are anxious over this responsibility. Recognize that how you cope with the anxieties of raising your child can determine whether you'll be successful or unsuccessful parents.

Less successful parents tend either to avoid their worries or remain lost in the "work of worry"; they worry constantly but never do anything about the things they are worried about. Successful parents, on the other hand, anticipate the problems of child-rearing and plan appropriate strategies. Instead of remaining lost in worry, successful parents plan ahead and are ready to deal effectively with problems that occur. Because they are prepared, successful parents develop confidence and feel good about themselves and their off-spring. These feelings of well-being foster the development of a happy and healthy family situation.

You must begin to anticipate how you will respond to anxious thoughts that may cross your mind. Be prepared! Because you are reading this book, you are probably interested in your child's being coordinated, athletic, and happy. How will you respond if at 8, 10, or 15 years of age all the children in the neighborhood are more coordinated and athletic than yours? What if your child shows no interest in sport or exercise? What if your child is afraid to catch a ball? What if highly skilled running and throwing develop late? You must be prepared to address these questions.

Summary

Raising a child athlete can be difficult but rewarding. Remember each of the following points to help you deal with the challenges you will face in the years ahead.

- Unconditional love is necessary for the healthy growth of your child.
- Providing positive sport experiences for your child is one of your primary responsibilities.
- Encouragement is more motivating than discouragement.
- Your child must eventually be able to think for himself or herself and to know right from wrong, but in the meantime discipline is crucial.
- Spoiling a child leads to weakness rather than strength.
- Role modeling, provided by your own participation and encouragement, is usually the greatest source of learning.
- Disappointments never killed anyone, but they make successes feel great.
- Empathy builds strength; sympathy breeds weakness.
- Confidence grows faster from remembering successes than failures.
- Even the toughest athletes cry and sometimes feel like quitting.
- Happy athletes play better than unhappy athletes.

- Winning isn't everything, and it isn't the only thing. Winning should be enjoyed and appreciated when it occurs, but your child must realize that losing is also part of sport.
- Athletes will have more failures than successes during their careers unless they always play opponents who aren't as good as themselves.

Life as Parents of an Athlete

Chapter 2

So it looks as if your child is going to be an athlete. What can you expect? Will life be different as your child's involvement in sport continues? You bet it will, and you need to get ready for what lies ahead. You will have to make many adjustments in your schedule and priorities, but if you believe in the value of sport, the changes will be worthwhile.

Special Demands of Raising a Child Athlete

When you decide to encourage your child to participate in sports, you will have to adjust in several ways. You will have to adjust the family schedule to fit the sport's demands; you will have to take special care to see that no one in the family is neglected because of the athlete's needs; and you will have to put special effort into maintaining your own commitment when the child's career is not going as well as planned.

A Different Way of Life

You and your family may need to live on a different schedule and at a different pace if your child becomes a serious athlete, depending upon your child's sport and level of commitment. Year-round sports such as swimming and tennis may be more demanding than others such as football and softball, which generally entail only one season of upheaval. However, more and more sports are gradually moving toward a year-round commitment. Every season is "in season." Practices and competitions are frequent and often occur at distant locations.

Some days you may come home from work feeling tired and in a bad mood, and you won't feel like doing anything with a loved one, much less what some expert has suggested. Some days your child will feel the same way. Occasionally, neither you nor your child will feel well. You must accept these days as a part of being human.

Your ability to prepare for and joyfully live with your child's pace and schedule will be crucial to your child's success and happiness. If you wish to make the sport experience a positive one, you must be willing to make some sacrifices. In doing so, you must think positively and avoid complaining, especially in front of your child. Children are perceptive.

A parent's job can be very demanding in today's sports world. You may start feeling sorry for yourself if your child gets deeply involved in sport, and you may have every right. A typical parent-child dialogue in your home each evening may go something like this:

Child: *Don't forget we've got to get up at 4:30 a.m. We've got to get to diving lessons by 5:30. Coach will be upset if we're late. I need time for a good breakfast. What are we having? Then we need to get to school for first period. I'll need a good lunch. We'll need to meet right in front of school at 3:20 so we can make it to afternoon practice. Can you get me some new socks at the store while you're waiting? I hope dinner will be ready when we get home so I can do my homework and get to sleep.*

Parent: *All set! But make sure that you've set the table for both of us. Be sure to make your bed after you get up in the morning and put your dishes in the dishwasher after breakfast. And be sure to be ready to go on time. You take responsibility for getting yourself up, and if I'm not up, be sure to wake me. I have lots of other errands to run this afternoon. Make sure you are where you're supposed to be at 3:20. I won't be able to wait. Okay. Good night.*

What's a parent to think? Does this child think you have noth-ing to do but cart him or her around town? It will take lots of love. You will have to work hard to avoid spoiling your child. You will have little time for yourself, and when you finally have free time, you will be ready to collapse. Heaven help your spouse or other children!

If your home is far away from the school, pool, club, or gym-nasium, you may begin and end many of your days as a chauffeur. But this may be just the beginning. You will be asked to be a nutri-tionist, athletic trainer, psychologist, masseur or masseuse, and wash-and-dry specialist. You will spend much of your time learn-ing about each of these areas to fill these roles. You must be ready for a different lifestyle—one that is busy, exciting, and unusually satisfying.

Treating Each Child as a Special Person

A highly motivated child athlete will require special attention and understanding. The desire to achieve and the need for success will cause many moments of exhilaration and discouragement. When excited, the child may dominate family conversation with interest-ing stories of success. When discouraged, the child may seek sup-port and attentive ears from parents and siblings.

Parents may easily get caught up in the life of their child athlete, which may appear to be more interesting than the lives of other children. Parents of a successful child athlete may receive an abun-dance of social support in their community as well.

Parents must give time and attention to their young athlete, but they must also regularly remind themselves of the need to give "quality" time to their other children. They must encourage and support the interests of their other children even if those interests are not as publicly stimulating and popular. The other children in your family must know that they are loved and that you are equally proud of them.

The challenge is greater when siblings are not as highly motivated or in need of parents' time and energy as the child athlete. It is easy to feel disappointed in these children, wondering what is wrong with them for not being as ambitious and goal-oriented as their athletic sibling. Nothing is wrong! They are normal children who need and deserve as much love and attention as the child athlete, even if they don't ask for it. These children will need frequent support and encouragement for every little success or striving. If you fail to sup-port and encourage *all* of your children, sibling rivalry may result. Children react to such rivalry in many different ways. One child may think that a sibling will always be better at everything and therefore give up even trying to compete. Another child may seek out a different sport or nonsport activity. Another may work twice as hard to live up to the family reputation. Some children may respond with admiration for the sibling, while others may grow jealous and bitter of the extra attention the child athlete receives.

In a family where an older child has been successful, the pressures on a younger child may be especially burdensome. The problem may be longlasting because the comparisons and references to the sibling may never end.

Evelyn Johnson, the younger sister of NCAA and NBA star "Magic" Johnson, found his act hard to follow despite being an outstanding player in her own right, as reported in a *Sports Illustrated* story (Jackson, 1981):

> After two seasons at South Carolina, Johnson, now known as Sweet E around the Columbia campus for her fluid, yet powerful style of play, has an identity of her own. It didn't come easily. When she arrived at South Carolina in the fall of '79, most everyone she met asked the same annoying question—What's it like being Magic Johnson's sister? Magic Johnson's sister would sometimes reply with disgust, "I don't know. He's just like any other brother. But a little richer." He may have been like any other brother to Evelyn, but to the fans who were all too aware of her family ties, only a Lady Magic would do. "I felt the pressure of being his sister," Evelyn says. "I thought everyone wanted me to go out and perform the way he did. I felt I had to do *everything* right." (p. 82)

As a parent, you must be alert to signals that your child is struggling with sibling rivalry. When you suspect a problem exists, take advantage of every opportunity to show love to your child. In addition, when you are alone with your child's friends, tell them how proud you are of your child. Such a message, which is sure to get back to your child, may be even more powerful than a message given directly to him or her. A child who is insecure or uncertain about how a parent thinks or feels often wonders during direct communication if the parent is sincere, and the impact is lost. In such situations direct communication supplemented with indirect statements to others who are likely to repeat them to the child can be the most powerful way to convey the message.

The father of a highly successful young baseball player named Tom explained to us how he handles this situation.

His sister Christine goes to college at the school where Tom is a star. His younger brother Ed is still in high school. Christine is an actress in school plays. I'm very proud of her, but no one else would know about her except for the fact her brother is a star. You might even assume she has an identity crisis. But when her drama teacher said, "Christine, this play is going to help you find yourself," Christine replied, "I didn't even know I was lost." What I do is make sure that all of our children know we feel the same about them no matter what they do. We love sport, but we remind the children it is just a game. Sport is important, but life keeps going on and we will always love and support them all.

The public attention and recognition accorded to athletes can cause athletes to expect and receive preferential treatment. Such special treatment is not always harmful, but it may lead to family conflicts and concerns. Parents must strive to make each child in the family feel special while emphasizing that being special may mean that a child is different but not more important than others. Parents should help each child to realize the need to try to make all of their sisters and brothers feel special by both words and actions. This is a family responsibility, and the family must come first.

Maintaining a Commitment to Sport

The demands of sport can be excessive in time, travel, and money. In the beginning, you may be able to coach your child yourself, but as your child begins to show talent, quality training programs can become quite expensive. You then must make a decision: Is putting your child into a high-level program worth the time and money? Is your child committed to training in the sport? Does your child really have talent, or is someone telling you he or she is talented just to make a living off of your child's interests?

Perhaps you are considering sending your child to a special preparatory school that is oriented toward a particular sport. Will the school be good for your child, or will it cater only to children who are destined for a national championship?

These are not easy decisions, and they are even more difficult when you have your own needs that must be met. It is not always fun to drive a child to a field, court, or pool for lessons and then sit and wait for two hours. Nor is it always enjoyable to spend every weekend driving to competitions. In many sports, however, you will have to do such things if your child is going to make it, unless some caring and dedicated coach does it for you.

Families with two or more children face even more difficulties. Each child may be playing a different sport, in a different league, on a different day, at a different time and place. Parents with several children often find that taking their children to lessons or practices is a full-time job. If they are lucky, parents find some time for themselves and their own pursuits.

You must carefully consider the time commitment required before getting your child seriously involved in sport. If necessary for your sanity, set down some guidelines with your child. Make sure your needs are also considered, because if you don't, you may spend your parenting years unhappy. Soon you may find yourself angry at your child for demanding your time. This may turn you and your child away from each other and from sport.

Many parents are more than willing to make this commitment for their child. This is especially true when a child is successful, the parents are getting recognition, and the child is grateful. When these elements are not present, however, a different situation may exist. The absence of even one of these elements may give parents reason to question their continued dedication to their child's interest in sport.

When your child is unsuccessful, you must believe the child will improve with time and your continued support. You must also remember that much more than winning can be gained from sport participation. Focus on the self-discipline and respect for persistent effort your child is learning. Emphasize the friendships your child is making. Find a way to convince yourself that your child will gain a great deal from his or her commitment and from yours. In other words, redefine success in terms of performance qualities instead of outcomes. If your child is not yet successful, you and other loved ones need to support each other until success is achieved.

A young woman who is a two-time All-American distance runner and a national 10,000-meter champion was a late bloomer. She shared some interesting thoughts with us on her parents' role in her development.

My parents have been very important in getting me started in sport and maintaining my enthusiasm. I have seen too many Little League parents who yell and scream at the opposing team, ridicule coaches, fault officials—anything to blame someone other than their child for a poor performance. This attitude becomes instilled in the child, and often the child becomes a poor sport for the rest of his life, believing that he can do nothing wrong. I've also seen the other extreme in which parents never find anything right in a child's performance. They are constantly nagging the child to produce more or perform better in competition. How can a child ever learn to enjoy a sport under such constant pressure?

The most important thing that my parents taught me was to enjoy sport participation. Sport is not a necessity. I was never forced into it. If you enjoy what you are doing and want to be good at it, then you have to work at it. "Nothing worthwhile comes easily" was a favorite expression of my mom's. This attitude was important to me because I never had an abundance of talent. I had to be more determined and work harder than others to be successful. I competed in running from the age of 10 to 14 without winning any race or doing anything especially noteworthy. I was as slow as molasses! But I sacrificed and outworked others with my parents' support, and finally I won a national championship.

My parents taught me to never look for excuses: not to blame others for poor performances, to take the responsibility for yourself. If you win it's because of your own actions, and if you win it's your own accomplishment. They also taught me to run for myself and for my own reasons, not anyone else's. They helped me to realize that I shouldn't look back and dwell on bad experiences because you can't change the past. Forget it, mark it up to experience, and move forward.

As a child, when I decided I wanted to start running, there was no hesitation on my parents' part. The money for all those running shoes I went through was never denied, or at least it was never discussed in front of me. To run I needed shoes, and that was that. All those weekend trips up and down the coast to run in meets took a lot of time and money. Yet it was never an issue. The nationals seemed to be held on the other side of the country every year, but I was never denied the chance to compete. Don't get me wrong. I don't come from a wealthy family by any means. But somehow my parents always found a way. All they ever asked from me was to be truthful to myself, to enjoy what I was doing, and to work hard.

There were many times when I needed simple love and understanding, and my parents were always there. I can remember
coming home one night after practice in tears because things
were not going well. Mom asked me, "Do you still enjoy it? Nobody is forcing you to run, so if you don't want to, don't think
that Dad or I want you to." There are probably not many parents who would say that to their child when they loved to see
their child run and the child had won several national titles and
a full college scholarship.

To show you how much love such a statement took, you must
realize that my mother comes to all my races and yells like
crazy for me. I don't believe there is anything in life that gives
her more pleasure than watching me. Yet surprisingly, she has
never pushed too hard. She has made it clear to me that I must
run to please myself, not other people.

Parents who have a talented child must be sure not to force the
child to participate. A lasting and healthy attitude must be developed early. If sport is not a fun and positive experience, nobody is going to work hard or stick with it. The more disciplined
and regimented practice needed for improvement can come
later. Gifted athletes need to have a way out. They must know
that merely because they are good at a certain sport and have
accomplished great feats does not mean that they *must* continue playing. Continuing to play must be the child's decision.
If a child wants to quit, that should be okay, and the parents
shouldn't hold a grudge.

My parents are always there when I need them. If I win or lose
they are there to congratulate or console me. Nobody can play
a substitute role of a parent. Only they can have certain im-
pacts. Granted it must be a challenge. I think mine have
handled it splendidly!"

Our discussions with successful young athletes have led to several
suggestions. The following list is compiled from many interviews
and conversations with sport personalities. They suggest that parents take these steps:

- Help instill and maintain enthusiasm.
- Avoid criticizing or finding fault with your child, officials,
  coaches, or competitors.
- Don't try to force your child to love sport by nagging.
- Encourage persistent effort and believe that your child is ca-
  pable (crucial to late maturers).

- Foster self-responsibility and discourage excuses.
- Provide your aspiring athlete with opportunities.
- Remind your child to compete because he or she wants to, not because you want him or her to do so.
- Be there with your child after disappointing losses to understand and console, and to give the child the enthusiasm to start over again tomorrow.

Sometimes, despite your efforts, your child may not show appreciation for your involvement in his or her career. You then owe it to yourself and your child to have a talk. Tell your child about your needs. Explain what you expect from the young athlete and what he or she should expect for himself or herself. Begin early to teach your child there is a time for selflessness as well as a time for selfishness. If your child doesn't immediately understand, be patient, and don't quit on him or her. Continue to talk with the child. You will both grow and learn from the experience.

Special Family Problems

Two types of families may have special problems in connection with the child athlete: the single-parent family and the dual-career family.

The Single Parent

Single parents have special problems and pleasures raising child athletes.

If you are a single parent, it may be especially difficult if you were not an athlete yourself but would like your child to be active, coordinated, and confident. Remember, your support and guidance are more important than your physical skills.

One advantage you have as a single parent is that there is no disagreement over the rules of daily behavior for your child. You are the authority. But you alone must fulfill all the other roles and responsibilities as well, which makes the job tougher.

Regardless of the demands, the challenge for you as a single parent to raise a child-athlete can be an unforgettable experience. A key element in meeting the challenge is close rapport and constant communication. The struggle of sport competition will evoke a wide array of emotions in your child, but if you are alert, you will be able to read these emotions from your child's face and body. Even if you are totally lacking in technical knowledge about sport, you still can lend an ear to listen and a shoulder to lean on as effectively as anyone, and that is what young athletes need most. Whether such communication takes place in person or via the telephone, sensitivity, empathy, a willingness to listen, and a few words of encouragement are most powerful. As evidence, look at the rosters of the National Basketball Association and the National Football League and see the numerous players who were raised by single parents—primarily mothers.

Single parents who lack knowledge or interest in sport have many options. Finding a friend, relative, or neighbor to play with your child is one effective strategy. You can further assist your child's development by reading about sport, watching televised sport, and talking to others about sport. Speak with adults who have been athletes or coaches. Strive to develop an understanding of sport.

If they fail to recognize the importance of healthy competitive attitudes, noncompetitive single parents sometimes have difficulty bringing up athletes. A noncompetitive attitude is at least as bad as the too-competitive attitudes of many sport enthusiasts. You must help your child discover a healthy and balanced attitude toward competition.

It is not uncommon for a young athlete to quit sport soon after the parent who pushed sport leaves the family. The child may think the only reason for playing was to please the parent, and thus choose to quit. At this time it is useful to sit down with your child and discuss other reasons for playing sports.

Many athletes develop close and special relationships with their coaches. Often the coach becomes a second parent. The coach's influence is far reaching, and it is especially important for the single parent to get to know the coach, discuss values, and let the coach know his or her help is desired and appreciated.

Some single parents mistakenly look to their child as a confidant. But a preadolescent child is not yet ready emotionally or intellectually to fill this role. At this age, children still need a parent and guider. Single parents must look elsewhere for their own personal support, at least until their child is mature enough to fill this role.

Single parents can and do raise happy and successful athletes. However, this can only happen when they do not push their children for personal reasons, and when they remember that, while the child may seem to be much like an adult in his or her level of commitment, he or she is still a child.

Dual-Career Couples

Couples are increasingly choosing to pursue dual careers. In such families, it is not uncommon for a child to have little time with mom and dad.

Often dual-career couples are caught in a contemporary crunch. They love their children, but they may have limited time because they value other things as well, such as time for themselves, material goods, status, and their careers. There is little doubt that the economy is partially responsible for this dilemma. Dual-career couples attempt to balance the demands of a job and their desire for personal fulfillment with the responsibilities of bringing up children.

If you are part of a dual-career couple, it is especially important that you set aside some specific time to be with your child. One way is to do something for your child that the child could do for himself or herself, even if it means making breakfast or taking the child to sport practice. This will communicate to your child that you really care.

If your schedules make it impossible to spend much time with your child, you must make sure you regularly provide "quality" time. This means time especially set aside for your child during which your only thoughts are of your child and his or her interests.

Supporting the Family

Because of the pressures put on the family by your child's pursuit of sport, it will be extremely important for you to develop family interactions that are supportive and that help maintain clear communication. This section provides some suggestions on how to promote a positive, open family atmosphere.

Help Each Child Feel Good

Each child can develop a positive and realistic self-concept. All children acquire a sense of who they are, what they are capable of doing, and how they look as a result of their experiences and the way others respond to them. Children learn about themselves by their own actions and by their interactions with others.

One way to help children develop a positive self-concept is to treat each child as a unique individual. Accept your child for what he or she is, as well as what he or she is capable of becoming. This acceptance requires you to show that you care about your child by helping when help is needed, showing affection, and demonstrating genuine concern for the child's well-being.

If you provide clear and fair rules and discuss your beliefs and values, your child will be able to function freely within defined limits. With this approach, your child will be able to test his or her own skills and abilities at making decisions—and in fact learn that he or she is capable of making them, and that he or she is a competent human being.

Be positive. Children learn to feel good about themselves when they think others feel good about them. Adults communicate their positive attitudes toward children in many verbal and nonverbal ways. For example, the following behaviors give positive support to children and help their self-concepts: smiling, winking, joking with them, praising them in front of others, playing or practicing with them, patting them on the back, and giving victory signs or thumbs up signals.

Children also feel good about themselves when they believe their parents genuinely care. For example, when you help your child readjust goals or plan new techniques or game strategies, or ask your child for an opinion, you indicate that you value your child as an individual.

These positive techniques are particularly important after your child feels he or she has performed poorly. Acceptance as an individual must never be dependent upon good performance, and the child must always be helped to feel important and accepted.

Maintain Open Communication

Good communication with parents will help children enjoy sport. You must be able to show that you appreciate your child, value his feelings and ideas, and want him to enjoy sport. You should communicate your likes and dislikes and encourage your child to express himself freely.

If you are genuinely interested in your child, you will show interest both through verbal and nonverbal communication. You will motivate, encourage, and help solve problems and set goals through your communication with your child.

Be a Good Listener.   One of the most important skills in communication is the ability to listen. If you are a good listener, you will carefully tune in to what your young athlete says and does. When you listen, you are showing you care about the child.

There are several useful techniques you can use in careful listening:

- Nonverbal, attentive listening—Show through posture, facial expressions, and gestures that you are really paying attention.
- Invite clarification—Request a reexplanation or expansion of what your child has said.
- Paraphrase—State in your own words what you feel or understand has been said. This allows the child to reinterpret if he or she feels the point has been misunderstood.
- Restate—Repeat verbatim the last portion of what was said.
- Bridge—Indicate you are listening and understanding by interjecting bridge statements such as "I see," "yes," "uh huh."

A recent conversation between a father and his son illustrates these techniques in use:

Son: *Dad, I'm really scared about the opposing pitcher in today's game.*

Father: *Today's game?* (restating)

Son: *I get scared when I think about him hitting me with a pitch.*

Father: *I see.* (bridging)

Son: *Joe says he's really fast and gets real wild.*

Father: *So you're primarily concerned about him getting wild and throwing fast?* (paraphrasing)

Son: *He's really strong.*

Father: *You're strong and quick and a good hitter. Why does he bother you so much? You've hit well against other pitchers faster than him.* (clarification)

Son: *I'm afraid he'll strike me out or hit me.*

Father: *Remember you've been working on staying in the box and hitting aggressively. You're a good athlete. You'll get out of the way automatically if you have to do so. You'll react faster if you are confident and just believe in yourself. Go up there looking for a pitch to hit and watch the ball.*

Notice how well this parent used the positive approach to open communication. He used paraphrasing, clarification, bridging, and restatements to help build a sense of understanding with his son. As a result, the son will begin to sense the confidence his father has in his ability.

Have Open Discussions.   Keep discussions between you and your child open, even if your points of view differ. There are many ways to discuss the differences when you disagree. A recent case may illustrate this point. A 12-year-old player, Tom, lost in a local tennis tournament, but his friend was the champion. The friend announced he was going to the regional tournament, and Tom began a campaign to convince his parents he was good enough to compete in the tournament too.

His parents had two choices in combating what they perceived to be an unrealistic perception. They could have flatly rejected the trip to the regionals, which might have made Tom look bad in the eyes of his friend. However, they put themselves in his place, and opted to indicate that they felt he was developing into a fine player, but that there were some other things he might want to think about before deciding whether to attend the tournament. They then asked him several questions: Are you sure you will benefit more from going to the tournament than you would from staying home and practicing? Do you want to go to the tournament to compete, or do you want to go for social reasons—just to be with your friends or to be able to say you went to the regional tournament? How will you feel if you're not playing after the first round and your friends are and you have to stay all week without being able to play? They concluded by saying, "If you feel that you will benefit from going and will enjoy yourself all week, regardless of what happens once you arrive, you may go to the tournament. Take a day or two to think about these things and then make up your mind. It's your decision!" This technique works very well in a variety of situations.

A second example may help to clarify the use of this successful technique. A volleyball coach encourages the team members to offer suggestions about strategy. They suggest a new formation for the block. The coach allows them to actually try their suggestion and see if it works. This gives the team confidence that the coach really does listen to them, and if the new formation works, the whole team benefits. If not, the coach can use it as a teachable moment and explain why it did not work.

If you show an individual you are considering his or her opinions, you will find it much easier to express differing views. Several techniques other than trying the suggestion might be employed. One is simply talking about the child's ideas. Try approaches that include such phrases as "I like your thought, and there are many things you have said that I agree with. However . . ." or "I can see why you feel the way you do. But there might be another way to think about that."

An alternate technique employs the well-placed pause. You may often be tempted to jump in with an immediate "No, you can't" or "That's not right, it won't work." You will be much more effective if you pause. Your silence may indicate that you see what your child has in mind and are at least thinking about it.

You must realize that giving children the right to express their opinions fosters self-reliance, self-responsibility, and ultimately the ability to think for themselves. These are important in providing chances for children to learn to trust themselves.

Accommodating Sport Training Needs

Besides the psychological adaptations the family must make to support the child athlete, there will be time and monetary demands to be met.

Transportation and Car Pools

Transporting your child around town or the state regularly is not an easy task. You are indeed fortunate if you live next door to the practice area. If not, chances are you will become a full-time transportation specialist. You may need to form a car pool to help you protect your sanity. Jane Stuart, a 14-year-veteran swim parent, suggests the following guidelines for forming car pools:

1. Realize that everyone will sooner or later mess up a car pool, so stay calm.
2. The driver for the day must be on time. No excuses are allowed for being late. You must prepare for problems.
3. If it is your turn to drive, you drive, no matter if your child is going to practice that day or not.
4. You cannot take two weeks off whenever you get tired of driving. Athletes must get to practice.
5. A car pool is a cooperative endeavor and you have a responsibility to other members. You must make rules for your car pool and stick with them or get out of the pool. Create guidelines and rules about allowable child behavior in the car. Be consistent in discipline.
6. Be certain to tell each child exactly where to be for pick-up and emphasize the importance of being ready. If they are not, leave them behind. (Stuart, 1978, p. 6)

Vacation Plans

You may have always thought vacations were crucial to family success and happiness. Perhaps you assumed that your entire family felt the same way. Watch out—you may be in for a rude awakening.

Your child, and your child's coach, may not agree with your vacation plans. In a coach's mind, vacations often interfere with physical and mental preparation. Your child's coach may believe you don't care or understand if you take a vacation when practice is scheduled. Successful coaches do not see holiday seasons or summer as vacation times, but rather as opportunities to get more quality practice time out of their young athletes. You must realize that a coach may lose interest in you and your child if you insist on taking vacations and missing practices.

If you want to do what is best for your child, discuss with the coach the ideal time of year to vacation. Do not assume vacations are bad for your child; they are probably important to your child and to the entire family. But pick an appropriate time. Find out if your child is expected to work out while on vacation, something many coaches will expect as a minimum. If workouts are impossible, you and your child may need to decide whether to leave the child at home with a friend or the coach while the family vacations. In making decisions, try to understand the coach's view and its impact upon your child's development. You must, of course, balance this need with your family's needs.

Expenses

How much does it cost to raise a child athlete? No one really knows. It varies from sport to sport, but you can be sure of one thing—it will be expensive. The entry fees, the cost of gas, the doctor bills, the cost of equipment, shoes, and clothing are never ending. Every athlete feels he or she must have the best equipment to have "the edge."

Expenses for equipment can be a major financial burden. Consider the cost in rackets and strings alone for a top junior tennis player. Bjorn Borg went through 300 sets of gut and about 150 rackets per year. Fortunately, as your child improves, equipment manufacturers may provide free equipment.

As you may already be aware, equipment is constantly updated and improved, particularly in individual, nonschool sports. The cost of special lessons can be enormous. You also may find yourself spending money on instructional books, cameras, and videotapes.

Lost or stolen equipment increases the costs needlessly for many young athletes. The following suggestions can help you cut down on this problem:

1. Put a name tag on everything.
2. Force your child to try to track down lost items.
3. Let your child know the consequences of lost or stolen equipment. It may mean doing without equipment for days or weeks until the equipment is found or money is earned to replace it.
4. Find a safe place for storing equipment.
5. Develop a habit of checking for equipment before leaving a practice or competitive site.

When purchasing equipment for a young child, parents would do well to buy one or two grades below the top of the line. Usually there is little difference in quality and a great difference in price. Another alternative is to buy at the end of the season, when you get discount prices. If your child is highly successful, feel comfortable about calling manufacturer's representatives and asking for free equipment, or have a coach make the call.

Summary

Life as a parent of a young athlete will be full of challenges and choices. You must anticipate possible stresses and plan successful ways to handle them.

The demands on time, energy, and financial resources will be great. Developing the ability to talk about and handle these possible changes in family priorities requires good communication. Sharing your values and expectations will be important to establishing a good sporting family life. Treating each child as a special person is essential and requires giving reinforcement to the athletes and their siblings.

Some of the most important contributions parents can make to their children include instilling confidence and self-trust by emphasizing hard work and effort and providing opportunities to accept challenges and responsibility. This will require good communication, both verbal and nonverbal. Such open discussions and unconditional love will build a positive, supportive environment.

Choosing the Best Sport Experience

Chapter 3

Children participate in sport for many reasons, some of which may change with age. Some children have a strong desire for social acceptance; they may need to please others or to be part of a friendly group. Others participate because they want to excel; they seek personal improvement and mastery of skills or other individuals. Still others seem to participate for the pure love of it; they enjoy the excitement and sensory stimulation that is part of sport.

Young children tend to be motivated by their social desires. These children enjoy working toward goals and strive to be liked and accepted by their peers as well as their parents. If your young athlete is primarily attracted to sport for its social value, encourage the child to invite team members to your home, talk with other children, organize "pick-up games" and practices, and take advantage of other social opportunities that sport offers.

As children grow older, many become motivated primarily by their desire to achieve. They seek chances to test their skills and enjoy being evaluated. They like to beat other people and standards of performance. Children who grow up being successful at realistic tasks continue to strive to challenge themselves. Early successes are critical to developing achievement-oriented individuals.

Some children are motivated by the sensations of sport. They enjoy sport because it "feels good," or excites them, or changes their mood. Adults who love to jog may understand this attitude—jogging is relaxing, provides a change of pace, and generally makes them feel good (at least when it's over!).

Why Children Quit Sport

Your need to understand these reasons for participation is especially important as your child grows old enough to enter the world of organized sport. A child probably has as many reasons for quitting sport as for entering sport:

- Other interests
- Not getting to play
- Negative reinforcement and criticism
- Frequent or constant failure
- Lack of money for further participation
- Competition against other children of unequal size
- Fear of injury
- Dislike of pressure
- Perceived lack of ability
- Overorganization of sport by adults

Many children drop out of sport because they develop other interests. Highly committed athletes, however, tend to quit when they start losing regularly. Other activities become more attractive to them because an overemphasis on winning causes them to question their interest in sport. This is a good reason not to emphasize achievement and a serious approach to sport until your child is ready.

If you understand what attracts your child to sport, you will be better able to help the young athlete enjoy the experience. Some parents find that a series of questions will help generate conversations about sport with their child. For example, the following questions guided a recent conversation with a young basketball player:

What do you like about basketball?

Why did you decide to play in this league?

What do you hope to get out of playing?

What specific things would you like to accomplish this year?

How will you go about accomplishing them?

Is there anything about basketball you don't like?

What would make you quit?

How do you like others to respond when you do something very well? Very poorly?

What kind of practices do you like?

When you have a new skill to learn, what makes you work hard to master it? What would make you give up?

How important is winning to you?

Would you rather sit on the bench for a winning team or play regularly for a losing team?

Questions such as these may help you identify your child's particular interests and allow you to help your child choose appropriate sport experiences.

A Specialist or "Jack of All Trades"?

Should your child specialize in one sport early in life? Should your child play many sports? Should your child specialize in sport alone or will academic success and an active social life also be important?

There are definite advantages to being a "jack of all trades." A child who plays many sports will have the opportunity to learn many skills and compete in many areas. The negative effects of failure in one sport are far less devastating when there are other activities in which your child can experience success. The major disadvantage is the present emphasis on specialization in the sports world, which makes it difficult to attain success or even make a high school or college team without specializing. The well-rounded individual must compete directly against others who have chosen to specialize. Unless a child is a gifted athlete, playing many sports may reduce his or her chances for success.

The Well-Rounded Athlete

Well-rounded child athletes will be better able to choose sports they enjoy the most and in which they have the most talent. They can choose to specialize in a single sport in high school or college if they want to or have to do so. The well-rounded athlete will more than likely have a balanced identity. Whether a formal athletic career ends with junior high school, high school, college, or professional sport, your child won't be so likely to suffer an "identity crisis" resulting from loss of competition.

Dan Jones, who played at Lewis and Clark College, Portland, Oregon, is a good example of a well-rounded athlete. He played varsity basketball, baseball, and football. He shot better than 50% on field goals in basketball, batted .384 in baseball, and was a National Association of Intercollegiate Athletics honorable mention All-American football player. He has suggested that playing multiple sports is an important experience for all of life. In particular, he suggested in a *Sports Illustrated* interview (Moore, 1981) that each sport is unique in its demands on concentration.

> A football game is the most intensely exciting for me. You build up all week for a single game, while in baseball or basketball you play all the time. Also football demands a clearer head. You're using called plays, each with an exact number of steps and moves, so it takes more discipline than basketball where the thing is flow and reacting to developments. Baseball is relaxing. You hit and field and have a good time. . . .
>
> Looking back, I can see how my sports have strengthened my willingness to take a chance. (p. 72)

Well-rounded athletes may wonder aloud how successful they might have become if they had chosen to "go for it" and specialize in one sport, but usually they are happy and well-adjusted. They are on their way to occupational and personal success while remaining physically active and healthy.

The Specialist

Far more problems appear to occur for young athletes who specialize too early, especially when they don't really love their chosen sport and give little attention to achieving academic success or establishing friendships. A recent case describes the potential seriousness of this problem. A 17-year-old athlete had dedicated his entire life to tennis and had become quite successful. His grades in school were Cs and Ds, yet he was unconcerned. He was sure he would either get a college scholarship or become a pro. The only peers that remotely resembled friends were other tennis players living around the state and the region in which he competed. During the spring of his senior year in high school, he suffered a career-ending shoulder injury. He first tried to learn to play with his other hand but eventually abandoned the idea. Later, two surgical operations were performed without success. For the first time, he realized no one cared about him. He didn't have any true friends. Tennis would not get him into college. He had no other skills with which to earn a living. Without tennis he felt lost and confused. His life appeared to have no meaning or direction because he had lost his ability to perform. He felt totally lacking in skill in other sports and initially was too proud to become a "beginner" once again. He felt he would only embarrass himself losing to others he considered nonathletic. Fortunately, with guidance and the support of his parents, he was able to find a new sport. He is now a happy and well-adjusted adult who participates regularly in recreational sport while putting the work ethic he learned in his years as a tennis player into practice in his job.

If your child is truly a gifted athlete, the issue of specializing versus playing a variety of sports may be irrelevant. An athlete who is talented enough may be able to start at any age and still excel. Kellen Winslow, the All-Pro receiver for the San Diego Chargers of the National Football League, played only chess and worked after school for United Parcel Service until the end of his junior year in high school. Then his physical education teacher noticed him and asked him to try football. He did, in his senior year, and went on to become a star.

Players like Kellen Winslow are the exceptions, however. For most highly motivated young athletes, the realities of today's sport world necessitate specialization at a fairly early age. You can help your young athlete avoid some of the pitfalls of early specialization by adopting the following guidelines:

- Help your child find at least one sport to play at a recreational level that can serve as a lifetime sport.
- Encourage your child to find time for academic success and socializing with the peer group, even though the chosen sport will take priority in terms of time and energy.
- Help your child develop an identity that does not require sport success.
- Help your child plan to take breaks from sport.
- Encourage your child to realize that the "price you pay for success" does not require sacrificing everything else in life.
- Tell your child that it is fine to take sport seriously, but not so seriously that it isn't fun any longer.

Team Sport or Individual Sport?

Which is best for your child, a team sport or an individual sport? What is your child likely to learn from each kind of sport?

Team sports are useful for teaching your child to cooperate with others. This cooperative effort typically demands selfless behavior for the good of the team. Players who are not getting to play regularly may be making a sacrifice that is difficult to manage, but they are learning a valuable lesson that can be useful throughout life.

A young athlete must learn to listen to and obey commands from authoritarian coaches in many team sports, especially traditional and large-group sports. Discipline will be imposed by the coach. While useful, this may not be the best way for your child to learn self-discipline. This team orientation will also not leave you or your child much control over traditionally defined sport success. You will have basically two choices. Your child can adjust to the coach and earn the coach's confidence, or, if you can afford it, you can move your child to another school or another team. Seldom will the coach be the one who changes.

Success or failure are not judged in terms of individuals in team sports. Team success or failure is the key to goal attainment. Gifted athletes must learn how to use their physical skills as well as their interpersonal skills to influence team success. Less talented players learn the importance of maintaining supportive attitudes when it is easier to be self-centered and feel sorry for themselves.

Individual sport athletes must either coach themselves or seek out and hire their own coach. When coached, individual sport athletes are often given more leeway to discipline and direct themselves. Either way, athletes will quickly learn that their success or failure is in their own hands.

An ideal approach for your child might be early experiences with team sports later combined with individual sport participation. The child may especially benefit in the long run if one of the activities is a lifetime sport.

A More Popular or Less Popular Sport?

There are many sports available to your child. Which ones should your child play? Should it be the current "in sport," or one for lifetime participation?

There are more popular and less popular sports, and athletes who are successful in the popular sports get far more public and peer recognition. Stars in minor sports are virtually unknown in most communities, a situation that can be frustrating and discouraging to a young athlete.

The majority of talented athletes in a community will participate in the popular sports because of the abundant rewards. As a result, the competition for team membership will be stiffer. Competition is usually weaker in the less popular sports, so the chances for success for your child may be increased.

You must weigh these considerations with your child's talent and interests in offering guidance. Keep in mind that popular sports vary by community. In general, basketball, soccer, football, baseball, and field hockey remain the most popular school sports. But there are areas of the country where swimming, skiing, tennis, golf, gymnastics, skating, equestrian, track and field, or other sports are popular and extremely competitive. Table 1 provides some pros and cons associated with various sport choices.

Table 1   Pros and Cons to Consider in Choosing More Popular or Less Popular Sports

Pros	Cons
Popular Sports	
1. Always a crowd watching	1. Every mistake or failure witnessed and criticized
2. Abundant peer and public approval	2. Can feel as if under a microscope
3. Higher prestige	3. Don't know if friends like them for *who* they are or for *what* they are
4. Best facilities and equipment provided	
5. Quality and intense competition	4. Face stiff competition
Less Popular Sports	
1. Mistakes or failures not seen	1. Their great performances and successes not seen
2. No expectations placed on them by others	2. Even "stars" unknown
3. Free from public pressure	3. Harder to train when no one seems to care
4. Less quality competition	
5. Easier to achieve success	4. Feel like second-class citizen

Sport for Achievement or Family Socialization?

There are many reasons for playing sport. Regardless of the reasons, a sport that parents and child enjoy playing together is beneficial because it enhances family time and interest sharing. This should not always be a primary factor in choosing a sport for your child, however. If you instill coordination and the joy of competition in your child, lifetime family competition will occur later. When sport interests coincide, as they often do in active families, an enjoyable situation may result.

However, sometimes the parents' sport interests and the child's differ greatly. Given the time demands on a child athlete, parents will have to become patient, somewhat selfless, and willing to give up some of the time normally reserved for personal playtime to provide opportunities for their child to play.

Sport and Your Child's Socialization

Regardless of what sport your child chooses, the demands of that sport may make it difficult for your child to have a normal social life. While your child will need opportunities to meet other children and make friends, there will be many times that social pleasures will have to be sacrificed in favor of training and competition.

Making Friends

Friends are very important to young athletes, who spend so much time practicing and competing that it is difficult to keep a normal social life. Many times athletes choose to be friends with each other even outside of sport. This is quite understandable. For example, a swimmer explains why swimmers like to socialize:

> Swimmers spend so much time together—four or five hours a day. They have to be friends. It is your social life. To do your best competitively you need the loyalty and encouragement of friends. You need them to push you.

> Just because a swimmer is out to win in a meet doesn't mean teammates and kids from other clubs can't be friends. Once you're out of the water after a race, you congratulate or console each other.

> The Golden Rule still applies to swimmers. You don't hurt other swimmers, and you don't want them to hurt you. You want to swim your best, and you want your friends to swim their best. (Browning, 1980, p. 50)

Athletes in some high-level sport programs such as golf and tennis do not train and compete as team members. Children involved in such sports may become skilled at talking with adults such as parents and coaches but lack skill at interacting with fellow competitors. At tournaments, such children may compete, shake hands, and leave. At school, they may be isolated from their peer group because they must rush off to lessons at a distant location as soon as school is over. If this is the case with your child, pay special attention to his or her *social* development. It will be worth the effort.

Team sport athletes usually come by friendships much more easily. They must work together and communicate in order to achieve success. The bus trips, locker room time, practices, and team meals on the road all provide opportunities for the development of close and often lifelong friendships.

Nonconformity With Peers

A child will naturally struggle with balancing the needs for individualism with the normal fears of rejection that come from being "different and special." Fortunately, sport involvement makes this sometimes difficult struggle seem relatively simple for athletes because most peers value athletics more than they admire many other activities during the school years. You must be aware this will not always hold true, however. There will be times when your child will ask whether the dedication to sport and the search for personal identity and fulfillment of potential are worth the effort.

Typically, your child athlete will be practicing while others are socializing. He or she will be going to bed early, worn out after a hard day of exercise and study, while classmates are up late watching television or socializing. Your child may be up early in the morning while others are sleeping late. He or she may be avoiding drinking and drugs, while these are an integral part of others' leisure time. Your dedicated young athlete may have limited or delayed experience with dating because of the chosen emphasis on athletics.

When your child is satisfied with his or her development, these are sacrifices that are happily made. But an unsatisfied and frustrated child may begin to wonder if the effort is worth it. The child may wonder because of fears of rejection by peers for nonconformity. The child knows full well that if he or she is not successful in sport, it may be hard to establish an individual identity or attain the peer support provided for conformists. You must be ready to encourage and support a child who is struggling with these conflicts. A child athlete needs to be reminded at this time that if achieving success in sport were easy, athletes wouldn't be admired and respected. It is a time to show that you are proud of your child's persistent efforts. It may also be a time to help your developing athlete realize that he or she may not really be missing out on much, and that satisfaction and enjoyment shouldn't necessarily be equated with winning.

Perhaps most importantly, this is a time to be an active listener. Savor this opportunity to get to know your child. Be sure to take time to help your child reevaluate involvement (reasons, values, goals, commitment) in sport, because an athlete gains a sense of self-control and self-direction each time commitment is reevaluated. Sometimes the athlete will change direction. Other times the reevaluation will simply remind the athlete how much he or she really loves sport. It is great for fostering increased self-motivation.

Summary

Choosing the best sport experience requires a great deal of insight and open communication. You must understand what motivates your child to play, and why he or she may prefer a certain activity.

The choice between specializing in one sport or participating in many may have far-reaching consequences. The well-rounded athlete will have more choices for successful participation as an adult, but may never have the concentrated time to be a champion in one sport. Neither of these situations is right or wrong, just different. And as long as the goals and values of the child match those of the experience, positive outcomes may occur.

Sport may put demands on your child's social life that are sometimes hard for him or her to accept. With your help, however, these problems can be minimized.

Getting Started
and Setting Goals

Chapter 4

What is the best time for your child to get seriously involved in sport? That's a question that will have a different answer for each child. While the earlier the child starts, the better the chance he or she will have to excel later, a child who is pushed before he or she is mentally or physically ready may find sport too frustrating or may never develop a true interest in a particular sport. That's why it is important to consider the child's maturity and desire to play before committing to a sport.

Once a child is ready to work on sport skills, he or she will need to know how to set specific and realistic goals. This is one of the most important skills you can teach your child, for it is applicable to any undertaking your child chooses.

Getting Started

Children should begin to develop sport skills in early life. This is not to say that we advocate focusing on your 6-year-old as a potential

Chris Evert, Jimmy Connors, Nancy Lopez, or Hank Aaron. Your intention should not be to develop the best tennis player, golfer, or baseball player, but rather to teach your child good general body movement, hand-eye coordination, and enjoyment of sport. Once these fundamental skills are established, your child will most likely seek opportunities to further develop sport activities.

A key to teaching your child any sport is to remember that in their world (and hopefully in yours) it is a *game*. Children are motivated to have fun and feel worthy. So when you and your child partici-pate, it must be a rewarding experience. Practice sessions should be filled with positive experiences and reinforcers. Comments such as "good," "fine," "much better," "great shot," should fill the air when you play with your child.

Practice sessions for your child should be filled with "indirect challenges." These activities motivate by encouraging your child to strive to improve each day and enjoy doing so. It is much better to motivate children by challenging them to be better than they were yesterday than to compare them with others. You are the moti-vator, and your child's desire to improve provides the needed ac-tion and perseverance. Challenge your child with questions such as "Can you make five baskets in a row?" "Can you drive the ball 50 yards today?" A young child needs to establish goals and to en-joy realistically striving for those goals.

These indirect challenges allow you to structure sport experiences to match the competence level of your child. If they do not match the abilities of your child, such challenges may be frustrating and discouraging.

Physically and psychologically, children mature each day. They learn who they are and what they are capable of becoming. Sport provides an excellent medium for exploring their abilities. But sport is not the be-all and end-all. Make your child feel good about him-self or herself by providing positive experiences in and outside of sport.

Unless your child expresses an unusual interest, highly special-ized and mandatory practice sessions probably should not be started before age 10. Of course, some children will be ready earlier and some not until much later. The key is to be sure that your child is not forced into lessons and practice. Too often, forcing your child into a structured sport experience can lead to an early loss of in-terest or quitting. Once the child expresses interest, however, be sure to keep practices exciting, challenging, and enjoyable. Simi-larly, if your child wants to play with you, do it. Encourage but do not force your child. If you want your child to like sport, create an atmosphere in which he or she wants to play and learn.

Be sure to reinforce your child for trying, no matter what the performance outcome. It is probably necessary to discuss sport skill strengths and weaknesses, especially if your child asks you to discuss them, but you might be better off to provide a good model, discuss your own strengths and weaknesses, and simply let your child follow your lead.

Children need to learn to enjoy competing, improving, and seeking their own level of excellence. Help your child compare his or her own present performance against past performance rather than against others. This is a proven, effective strategy for helping develop a positive and realistic self-concept. As a result, your child will be happier and much more likely to continue to desire to participate with and against others in sport.

Children Must Be Psychologically and Physically "Ready"

Many people believe children learn skills easier than adults. This may appear to be so not because children learn more rapidly, but because their desire to learn is high and because they do not have as many bad habits to "unlearn" or fears to overcome. You must, however, be sure that your child is both psychologically and physically ready to attempt a particular sport or skill.

Children must desire to learn and must possess the fundamental tools to acquire the skills. For example, in gymnastics, teaching the rings or sidehorse to a young boy with no shoulder strength would be very difficult. It would be equally difficult to teach gymnastics skills to someone whose interests and desires are on the basketball court.

You must, therefore, match particular skills with your child's physical capacities and personal preferences. To do so, consider the following questions:

- What are the unique demands of the skill?
- Does my child possess the background to accomplish the task, including physical requirements, cognitive and perceptual requirements, and prerequisite experiences?
- Does my child wish to learn the skill and devote the time and effort that may be necessary to master the skill?

If you determine the match between a particular skill and your child's readiness is not compatible, the skill must be reevaluated, altered, or left for another time. Fortunately, most adults can create excellent substitute skills. For example, the advent of Tee-Ball illustrates a modification of the game of baseball in light of the difficulty many young children have in hitting a pitched ball. In this case, the ball is put in play from a batting tee (similar to a giant golf tee or plastic pipe) as tall as the youngster's waist. The advent of the GLM (Graduated Length Method) of skiing instruction answered the difficulties individuals of all ages have in handling full-length snow skis. The currently popular tennis rackets that are large-sized or have a cut-off or short handle allow most people to achieve success more rapidly and consistently. These modified implements may later be exchanged for the regulation-sized equipment.

Don't expect your child to be ready for a particular sport by a particular age. Because each child represents a unique combination of prior experience, motivation, and maturation, it is impossible to specify ages at which all children will be "ready." The specific skills of each sport must be analyzed. In order to play baseball, a person must be able to throw, catch, bat, and run. These skills may be further broken down into the requirements of being able to track a moving object and coordinate the position of the body with the ball. Once these essential skills are identified, good learning environments can be designed.

You must also remember that the skills a child is ready for today may change in the future. For example, an early maturer may appear to be an ideal basketball center as a 10-year-old, but by the time the player is 12, the other children may have matured more or grown taller. Be sure to teach all of the skills of basketball, not just those of a center.

The implication of the readiness concept is great. All children should experience the skills required for all positions in a particular sport so at the appropriate time they will be ready to make a choice. This broad base of experience is important to the future of all skill development.

Children Should Compete for Their Own Reasons

When children compete, they should compete at their own levels and for their own reasons. At a recent championship soccer match, a father was observed consoling his son Billy after the team had lost 28-0. He was so concerned over the loss that Billy's reaction astounded him. Billy said, "It was the best game ever!" He had played more than usual and had taken six shots at goal—an all-time high!

This soccer game is an excellent example of the differences in perception between adults and children, or between any two individuals, even when observing the same event. The nature of the championship soccer game provided what might be referred to as objective competition, but as Billy demonstrated, competition is only important when a child attaches meaning or significance to it, which is referred to as subjective competition. In this case, Billy's "success" related to his increased playing time and shots at goal, while his father's view of competition defined success in the more traditional sense—winning.

Clearly, your child may view competition quite differently than you do. Concentrate on communicating with your child and understanding his or her view of sport so you can avoid making sport an extension of your adult viewpoint.

You should also keep in mind that eventually your child will learn to be competitive and to value winning over losing. The subjective nature of competition emphasizes the importance of experience and suggests that your child will learn to attach importance to competition as a result of observing how others respond to competition. Naturally, you want to see your child succeed, but you must not let your own desires and ego interfere with the enjoyment that the child needs for success. If your child is successful, it is easy to feel you are a successful parent; if your child does not succeed, or is less coordinated than others, you may feel as though you are a failure. You must separate your feelings from your child's performance. Otherwise, your motivation to provide experiences is based on your need to bolster your ego, at your child's expense.

Every Child Grows and Matures Differently

Children grow and mature at different rates. Everyone's biological clock runs at a different speed. One child gains weight first and then "grows up," while another gains height and then "grows into" his or her body.

Most children go through several growth spurts. They will double their size in the first 2 years, then grow at a more steady rate until puberty, grow rapidly in spurts until adulthood, and then cease growing. Some children experience the growth spurt as early as 8 years of age, but others do not experience rapid growth until the late teens.

The following letter from a once-young athlete is an excellent example of a young child's struggles with maturation and the tremendous impact of one important adult.

Dear Coach:

You won't remember me. It was just a few years back. I was one of those kids that turn out every year for freshman football without the slightest idea of how to play the game. Think hard. I was the tall, skinny kid, a little slower than the others.

Still don't remember? Well, I remember you. I remember how scared I was of you when you'd slap your hands together and yell "Hit!" I remember how you used to laugh at me and guys like me when we'd miss a tackle or get beat one on one in practice.

You see, you never let me play in a game. Once in a while, when you'd be giving a chalk talk to the first string, I'd get to play a couple of downs of scrimmage.

I really admired you. We all did. But now that I'm a little older and a little wiser, I just wanted to let you know that you blew it. I didn't play football after my freshman year. You convinced me that I didn't have what it took, that I wasn't tough enough.

I remember the first day of practice, when you asked for all the linebackers. I wanted to be a linebacker. The first time I tried to tackle someone I got my helmet ripped off. All I had done was lower my head and hit. No technique. No tackle.

You laughed. You told me I ought to be a quarterback, that I tackled like one. All the guys laughed. You were really funny.

Another time, after I became a guard, I missed a block—in practice, of course. The guy side-stepped and I wound up with my facemask in the mud.

"C'mon! You hit like a girl," you said. I wanted to hit. I wanted to tell you how much I wanted to hit. But if I had, you'd have flattened me because you were tough and didn't take any backtalk.

We ran the play again, and I hit the same guy a pretty good shot this time. When I looked at you, you were talking to another coach.

I'm the first to admit that I was pretty bad. Even if I had been coached on technique, I still would have been a lousy football player. I was one of those kids who was a couple of years behind my peers in physical maturity and strength.

That's where you messed up. I grew up. By the time I was a senior, I stood 6'5" and weighed 220. I couldn't fly, but I could run pretty well. That nonathletic freshman could now throw a baseball harder than anyone in the state. I was drafted and signed by a major league baseball team.

When my strength started to increase about my junior year, the varsity coaches drove me crazy with requests to turn out for football. I told them I didn't like the game.

"But why not? You're a natural!"

"I dunno, Coach, I can't explain it. Football is just not my game."

Looking back I really regret not playing football. It would have been a lot of fun. Maybe I could even have helped the team. But thanks to you, I turned against the game before I ever really got into it. A little coaching, a little encouragement, and who knows? I guess I'll never find out.

You're still out there, I see, coaching the frosh and sounding mean. I wonder how many potentially good athletes, kids that are a year or two behind, that you will discourage this year? How many of them will be the butt of your jokes?

It took me a while to learn that your "toughness" is meaningless. You're just a guy who played a little second string in college. So what have you got to be so tough about?

How sad. You're in a position to do a lot of boys a lot of good. But I doubt that you will. You'll never give up a chance to look "tough" and sound "tough." You think that's what football's all about.

I know better. (Brooks, 1976, p. 2)

This letter brings out many points that are as important for parents as they are for coaches.

- A child's physical stature, coordination, and success in sport are not consistent predictors of stature, skill, and success after maturity.
- You should always believe in your child.
- Never place limits on your child—they will probably hold your child back.
- No one is enough of an expert to know what a child is capable of doing.
- A young child admires his or her parents. Your word is often taken as gospel. Be sure to live up to the responsibility accorded that admiration.

- Don't think you can tell if a child will be a great athlete by looking at his or her body—what's inside is just as important as what's outside.
- Personal ridicule destroys rather than fosters motivation.
- It is not necessary to sound tough or look tough to be tough.
- If you must pass judgment, it is far better to overestimate than to underestimate a child's potential.

Experiencing growth spurts at different times creates many problems for young athletes. Some will feel tall and gangly, while others feel like "shrimps." Some 12-year-old boys will have the beginning signs of beards and look quite muscular. Others will still look like cherubs. The important thing to remember is that both of these are examples of normal and healthy boys.

The frustrations of growing up aren't all related to size. Comments such as "I can't control my feet," "I'm all arms," "My hands are gigantic!" are common. Growth occurs at different rates for different body parts. For example, a child's head doubles in size from birth to adulthood, and the legs increase to five times their length at birth. The legs and arms undergo much greater increases in length than any other body segment.

Many children experience the frustration of feeling very coordinated at one age and then growing suddenly and feeling as if they have "lost it all." This usually happens when the arms and legs have grown quickly, and the rest of the body must practice how to handle these longer limbs. This is a normal feeling, and if practice at sport continues, it will remedy itself. Help your child understand what is happening to his or her body.

An additional problem is that boys and girls mature at different rates. By the age of 6, most girls are more mature, and by 14 they are nearly 2 years older in terms of biological and structural age than are boys of the same chronological age. Many 10-year-old girls are taller and stronger than 10-year-old boys. The difference in size between adolescent boys and girls causes some complex social problems. The child who catches or throws better is usually admired by other children. Unfortunately, a difficult situation may develop if the more skilled child is a girl, and also a girlfriend or sibling. Fortunately, today's youngsters accept this situation more easily than adults, who grew up in a generation where sex roles were more stereotyped.

Parents of early maturing girls should be careful to avoid comments that may cause them to feel uncomfortable about their size, strength, or speed. Late-maturing boys will need encouragement that with time they will grow.

Late Maturers.   Tom Kite, the top money winner on the 1981 PGA Golf Tour, provides a good example of a person who overcame obstacles created by delayed success. The care and concern of his parents clearly played a major part in his ultimate success. When Kite was 18 months old, his father put his first golf club in his hand. They played together until he was six, with his father encouraging him to spend 12 hours a day on the golf course. By the time Tom was eight, it was obvious he was not going to be a very large boy. His father recalls:

> When Tom was eight or nine he told me he wanted to be a pro, and I was just sick. I thought I'd made a terrible mistake and wished I'd never introduced him to golf. He was so small I never thought he could make it. I kept trying to dissuade him. I told him how thousands tried to make it on tour. Tom's reply was, "Well, Dad, if one of them's going to make it, that one's going to be me." (Dennis, 1982)

Tom Kite kept working at his game. After practicing his long shots for several hours, he would move to the pitching area, and then to the putting green. When Tom was 16, his father took him to see Jay and Lionel Herbert, two top pros, and their advice was this:

> There is no way to tell if anyone could ever make it on tour. Give him every opportunity. If he doesn't have it, he will find out soon enough. But if you talk him out of it now, he will always feel in his own mind that he could have made it. He would never forgive you. (Dennis, 1982)

Some late maturers acquire great desire and good habits related to goal setting and hard work. The mother of NBA basketball player Jeff Lamp told us, "Nothing ever came easy for Jeff. He was never an instant success. He didn't even start very often. He couldn't shoot well and he made colossal fouls . . . but he was such a determined kid."

During the summer, Jeff Lamp would practice as often as possible. The gym would be open from 2 to 10 p.m., and he was almost always there. He would even take a bag lunch for dinner. He never had a summer job—only basketball. By the time he was in the eighth grade he was still on the bench.

But in the ninth grade, he got a chance to play, and eventually won Kentucky's "Mr. Basketball" honor and All-American honors at the University of Virginia before going to the pro ranks. His drive and determination, coupled with consistent practice, paid off.

The following are some helpful thoughts regarding late maturity.

- Late physical maturation does not mean an athlete is not highly talented.
- Girls tend to mature earlier than boys.
- It is next to impossible to talk children out of wanting something they want badly, so don't bother trying to do so even if a young athlete does not seem to possess the necessary physical attributes. Desire makes up for many liabilities.
- Young girls who are bigger than boys of an equal age need to be helped to feel comfortable and feminine.
- Late maturers need constant encouragement.
- Young boys who are worried that they will never grow up must be reminded that boys mature later than girls.

Early Maturers. Early maturers often seem to have an advantage in sports that tend to favor taller and stronger individuals. The child who grows tall at an early age or who is able to win easily during junior competition may run out of success, however. Sometimes the early maturer attains premature success without ever really developing the skills necessary for continued success. As other children grow, or their skills develop, the early maturer may begin losing. Because some early winners do not learn the values of hard work, goal setting, and persistence, they may become easily frustrated.

Parents of an early maturing child who is experiencing success would do well to do the following:

- Help their child realize the other children will someday also be big and strong and quick.
- Encourage their child to attach success to mental as well as physical abilities.
- Encourage and reward their child's effort and persistence.
- Help the child to gain confidence from early success, but be sure to take the child to other states or regions of the country to compete against other early maturers.
- Realize that constant success is sometimes as harmful as constant failure in terms of motivation.
- Demand the child maintain emotional control during competition.
- Do not allow the child to become spoiled.

The Clumsy Child. Many children seem to mature in height and weight well ahead of their actual age, but they need time to learn to adjust to their bodies, to develop coordination and agility. A parent recently asked me, "My son is 9 years old. Physically he looks like an 11-year-old, but his coordination is that of an 8-year-old. With whom should he play?"

If possible, your child should participate in sport experiences that match his or her skill level, rather than size or age level alone. Learning the basic skills is tricky. Find activities in which size is not the major factor. If you don't, your child may feel out of place because of differences in social, emotional, and mental maturity, even though physical size may be the same. Children ideally should be grouped based on all aspects of development: age, size, ability, and interest.

Competitive programs for children are available in almost all age and ability levels. Over 30 national organizations exist to supervise and arrange competition for children. In addition, thousands of local groups such as recreation departments, police athletic leagues, and church groups organize athletic activities. Add to these groups the school-sponsored programs, and the total provides competitive opportunities for half of all children under the age of 15, about 18 million youngsters. So if you feel your child is not having a good sport experience, look around until you find a suitable level of competition and help him or her enjoy the fun.

When Should Organized Competition Begin?

How can you best decide when your child is ready for competition? Should your child be a gymnast at 7? A soccer player at 8? A football player at 12?

There is no one best age for competitive sport. The American Alliance of Health, Physical Education, Recreation, and Dance has suggested several guidelines for children who mature at a normal rate. In the organization's book *Youth Sports Guide for Coaches and Parents* (Thomas, 1977) minimum ages are suggested for certain types of sport: noncontact sports such as swimming, tennis, track, and gymnastics—6 years minimum; contact sports such as basketball, soccer, wrestling, and field hockey—8 years minimum; and collision sports such as ice hockey and tackle football—10 years minimum.

The development of your child must govern the ideal age. The intensity of each of these competitive experiences should be moderate, as children need opportunities to develop skills first. Once the skills are developed, the level of competition can be increased.

If your child is constantly begging to compete, give it a try if there are no physical dangers, but once your child begins, look for the following telltale signs that he or she is not ready:

- Is constantly overtired at home
- Loses the joy of competing

- Sulks around the house a lot
- Accuses teammates of cheating
- Asks if he or she has to go to practice or games
- Always has an upset stomach before or after games

Traditionally, teenagers have excelled in some sports, especially figure skating, tennis, swimming, and gymnastics. An occasional youngster has made a mark in other sports—Marlene Bauer in golf, Steve Cauthen in horse racing, Bob Feller in baseball, Bobby Orr and Wayne Gretsky in hockey, Bob Mathias and Cheryl Toussaint in track and field. Today, even teenagers may be almost too old in some sports. For example, in 1983 two girls aged 16 and 17, Tracee Talavera and Julianne McNamara, were among the most successful gymnasts in the United States. They were training in Eugene, Oregon, with 55 other top gymnasts, 26 of whom were between 9 and 12 years old. They were all training for the 1984 and 1988 Olympics.

Some of these athletes will become Olympic stars. Some will quit because they want a more "normal" life, which is understandable when you consider that some of them must live away from home in order to be near their coaches or competition. Such social demands and the lack of emotional support from their families can really take its toll.

Should Boys and Girls Compete Together?

Children should have opportunities to compete against others of similar skill level. There is probably no biological reason pre-adolescent boys and girls cannot compete together; however, after puberty boys may be stronger and taller than girls. In some sports, the increased size of boys may be unfair and even dangerous for girls. Yet in many sports, children of both sexes can continue to compete into adulthood.

Another reality of participation by both sexes is that sometimes both boys and girls will lose. As a parent, you must not be particularly concerned if your son loses to a girl or if your daughter beats a boy because it is simply another competitive experience that young athletes must learn to accept. You must serve as an appropriate role model for your child. Be sure that you do not overreact when you are in competition with someone of the opposite sex!

Because all sports require skillful movement, a commitment to acquiring new skills, and a desire to achieve—positive attributes for both boys and girls—you must not identify particular sports as "masculine or feminine." Parents transmit their beliefs to their children through their comments and actions. Fathers, or males in general, tend to have the most influence over a child's view of sex-appropriate behaviors, especially the activity selection of sons. The views of mothers, however, either alone or in combination with fathers' views, are also important and must not be ignored.

Of particular significance is the potential severity of social sanctions based on activity selection for both boys and girls. Social pressure is especially strong for sons who demonstrate what have been traditionally thought to be sex-inappropriate behaviors. Some parents seem to be concerned that their sons participate in "masculine" activities but are willing to give their daughters freedom to choose from a full set of activities regardless of gender identification. It is important that parents discuss their values with their children. All children should have the opportunity to develop many different skills and the right to make choices about their sport participation.

Setting Goals

When your child is prepared to work seriously on his or her sport skills, you will need to teach an important skill that your child will be able to use in all phases of life: setting goals. The ability to set specific and realistic goals against which progress can be measured is a powerful tool for accomplishing any task. This section will show you how to teach your child this valuable skill.

Who Sets the Goals?

Should you always let your child set his or her own goals? What do you do if your child seems to be without goals?

It is unrealistic to expect all children to be capable of setting their own goals. If left completely on their own, some children would accomplish little or nothing. Parents must intervene if they are not happy with this attitude. Negotiating with the child is often helpful when this problem occurs. For example, a parent might say, "I'm not going to tell you what to do with your free time, but you aren't going to watch more than an hour of TV per day" or, "If you expect me to drive you to swimming and tennis lessons, you must be willing to practice hard!" Another effective negotiating strategy might be: "If you practice four days next week, I will play ball with you on Saturday and Sunday."

You must realize, however, that you can't force your child to have goals and that no one, not even a parent, can decide on another person's goals. Instead, use challenges to begin getting your child interested in setting goals. For instance, ask your daughter what she enjoys doing when she plays. If she responds, "I like juggling a soccer ball on my foot," you might ask, "How many times in a row can you juggle the ball?" If she responds, "I don't know!" ask "How many times do you think you can do it?" Challenge her to see if she can do it a specific number of times by a set date. Agree to a reward that *she* wants if she meets the challenge. If she fails to reach the challenge goal but has clearly tried and improved, be sure to let her know you notice and simply give her an extension date for getting the prize.

Be sure to help your child realize that there is more to the journey than the arrival. Emphasize setting challenges, any challenges the child enjoys, and trying to accomplish them to begin getting your child interested in setting goals.

Setting Specific Goals

Goal setting is a useful device for improving skills and especially for directing practice and play behaviors. For example, a young female basketball player and her parents recently devised a list of goals after some careful thought. A portion of that list appears in Table 2.

Table 2   Sample Goal List

Specific Goal	Specific Behaviors or Strategies
Shoot 5 of 10 free throws.	Practice daily for 30 min. Focus on arm extension.
Shoot 3 of 10 jump shots from 8 ft.	Practice from six different angles. Shoot jumpers in pick-up games three times per week.
Display sportsmanship (no arguing with officials).	Do self-evaluation after each game (parents provide positive reinforcement for good behavior or loss of free play time for bad).
Be a good team member.	Give positive reinforcement and help to teammates. Be on time or early for every practice and game.

Once goals have been established, it is important that you help the child follow through on them, reevaluating as necessary. Encourage behavior that is consistent with the goals and reward it with praise and positive reinforcement.

Setting Realistic Goals

A young athlete who has accurately assessed his or her personal abilities needs to learn how to set realistic goals. A recent experience with a young basketball player named John provides an example. John said to us, "I want to be a major university-level basketball player when I grow up. I really like playing and I'm pretty darn good. I'm a good competitor, I love to shoot, and I think I can make it. Can you give me any advice?"

Again further discussion, we made many suggestions to John. We began by saying "Dreaming of being great can be a wonderful place to start. No one really knows right now if your goals are realistic or not. But let's back up a bit . . . take one step at a time." We reminded John that he must first make his middle school, junior high, and high school teams, and that it will be important that he excel at least at the high school level to be considered for a scholarship. At the same time, we told him that developing academic skills also would be important.

John noted that he isn't tall, nor is anyone else in his family. He recognized that he must develop his skills as a guard—develop good passing, become an excellent dribbler and ball handler, and develop a solid outside shot—to have a chance at achieving his dream. We told him further, "Fortunately, these are all skills that can be developed through persistent practice. Based on your present level of skill, you will have to dedicate several hours per day to practicing these skills. Do you enjoy playing enough to do that? If not, you are simply dreaming and will be guaranteed failure and frustration because there are thousands of other young athletes around the country who want that scholarship. Some have less talent than you do, some just as much, others more. If these athletes improve more than you between now and then, they will get the scholarship."

It won't be easy for John. Getting there could be lots of fun, but there will be many frustrations. It was important for us to point out to John that even after all his practice, he may not make it. "Take a week and give some careful thought to these points. There are certainly sports easier to excel at than basketball. But if after looking at your abilities and desires relative to others, you still want to try, then let's lay out a practice plan and go after it," we told him.

Next we had John identify some goals and questions he had to answer before he could design a plan for practice. His long-term goal was to be a major university basketball player. Intermediate goals he would have to achieve would be to make the junior high team; start on the junior high team; make the high school team; start on the high school team; and star on the high school team. For now, his short-term goal would be to make the middle school team. Some questions he needed to think about were these: What are the required skills at the major university level? What is my present skill level? What level of commitment am I willing to make? How many hours a day will I practice?

We told John to outline a 6-year plan based on this information to take him from where he is now to where he wants to go. We told him to break each year into months, weeks, and days and plan what, how, and how long he would practice.

Some parents may find this advice a little pessimistic or cautious. It is simply realistic. It is important that you help your child consider these often overlooked factors when making decisions about where to focus efforts. You can help your child look at the available information, but ultimately the decision and commitment must be your child's.

Once your child makes a decision, be encouraging and optimistic. Don't second-guess your child's decision. Be supportive. But at the same time, remember that a goal is not set in concrete once it is established. If your child repeatedly comes home frustrated and discouraged, and after months or years of striving, improvement is lacking, you should help your child reevaluate the quality and direction of his or her efforts.

All effective competitors reassess their goals periodically to determine whether they overestimated or underestimated. This process will help your child determine which goals are realistic. Often, it is best to begin the reassessment by focusing attention on the direction of the goals: "Should I keep working at basketball? Can I attain my goal? Should I switch sports?" If the decision is made to continue, it is a good idea to focus on improving the quality and quantity of practice or to lower the specific goals slightly. Once these lowered goals are met, it will be easy to raise the goals once again and continue moving forward.

Adjusting goals is not giving up; it is keeping goals in line with capabilities. Adjusting goals will allow strengths, weaknesses, and improvements to be recognized. Goal setting will allow your child to learn how to turn dreams into reality. The result will be a happier and more motivated athlete.

Successful people in all walks of life set goals and maintain their motivation in striving to meet them. Setting an overall goal and then finding the best route to attainment through short-range goals is the key. Mark O'Meara, as a rookie on the pro golf tour, described his goals in the magazine *Sky* (Newman, 1981). His dream started when he was about 13 and he fell in love with golf while watching tournaments on television. He set a sequence of specific goals: learn the game, play in junior tournaments, earn a college scholarship, win the U.S. Amateur title, make it through the PGA qualifying school, and earn a player's card for the tour. His goals for the first year on the tour were to earn over $100,000, to finish in the top 60, and to be named Rookie of the Year.

Progress Charts

Recording progress on a chart can motivate a child who has set goals. Parents often use this technique to help children realize their changing height and weight by placing a simple measure on the wall and periodically marking a date near the new measurement. Charting helps because it visually indicates improvement, records information, and shows concretely that effort leads to forward movement.

Making progress charts is a simple technique that can be used for a variety of skills. For example, two parents recently came asking for advice about their two children, Kim and Billy. Both children wanted to develop their basketball skills. In particular, they wanted to improve their free-throw shooting, dribbling, and layups. We helped them devise a series of questions and charts to record the children's progress. These charts also helped them focus attention on the desired goals and provided positive feedback to the children.

The parents asked the children the following questions. If the children did not know the answers, they tried the activities to find the answers.

- How many free throws can you make in 20 attempts?
- How many layups can you make in 1 minute?
- How long does it take you to dribble half court and back? Can you do it by alternating hands on the ball—two dribbles with the right hand, two with the left?
- How fast can you run from the baseline to the closest free-throw line and back for five round trips?

After answering the questions, the two children, with their parents' help, decided on a series of challenges to measure their progress. The specific nature of these challenges can be modified to suit the needs of your child. The goals and target behaviors can and should be changed as each child acquires new skills. The charts in Figures 1 and 2 were developed for Kim and Billy. They were posted on the refrigerator so that the children could record their performance each day.

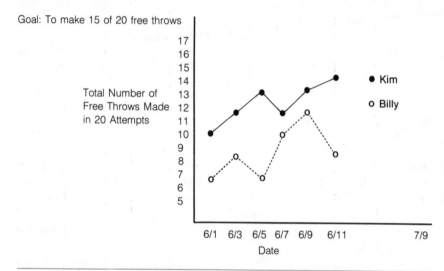

Figure 1.   Sample free throw progress chart.

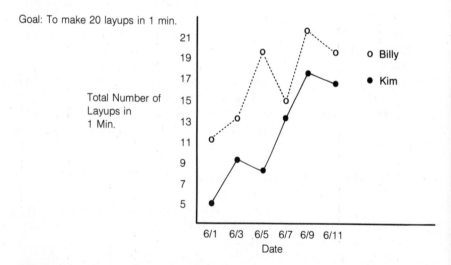

Figure 2.   Sample layup progress chart.

Keys to Goal Setting

The following suggestions may help your children set their own goals effectively and provide a guideline for designing and posting goals that will help direct practice.

1. Set long-term, intermediate, and short-term goals that will help attain a main long-term goal.
2. Develop and write down a strategy and schedule for attaining the main goal.
3. Be sure that goals are positive rather than negative; specify what you want to happen, not what you want to avoid.
4. Be specific whenever possible.
5. Imagine accomplishing the desired goal over and over. Dream about how good it will feel when it is attained.
6. Put a time frame on your goals but not a limit. Keep working at your plan.
7. If anything, underset your goals rather than overset them. As long as you reach your goal, you will be able to feel good about yourself and can then reset your goal to a higher level.
8. Share your goals with people who will help you attain them and be strong in resisting people who try to stop your progress or discourage your effort.
9. Write your goals down. Make a permanent record. Post them where you will see them often.
10. Reinforce your goals by reading them often. Remind yourself how important they are to you.

Remember, the best way to teach your child about goal setting is through your own words and actions. Use the same process to set goals for yourself. Show your child how much you enjoy setting goals and working toward accomplishing them. Let the child want to use this technique because he or she has seen the strategy bring you success and happiness.

Summary

All successful athletes have dreams, goals, and aspirations. In order for a child to become a star, these must become targets and desires.

Parents can help their child learn how to set appropriate goals. Setting realistic goals means structuring a path to the future through both short-term and long-term targets.

Goals cannot be used effectively unless the young athlete is ready and eager. They must fit the child's needs, not those of friendly adults. They must acknowledge the special, unique characteristics of each child.

Guiding Your Child to Competitive Success

Chapter 5

Teaching your child to be competitive and goal-oriented is not an easy process. There is no simple "how-to-do-it" formula. Children must strive to do their best but cannot be perfect at everything they do. Your child must experience some failure so he or she will learn and grow from the experience.

Competition is instructive if it is approached effectively. It can be destructive if approached ineffectively. The keys are

- to understand a process for effective competition,
- to develop a competitive attitude that sets a child up for success,
- to instill self-confidence,
- to develop the self-discipline and time-management skills required of student athletes, and
- to emphasize that values are important, and that to win without fair play is meaningless.

A Process for Effective Competition

Effective and healthy competitors like themselves. They have the challenge of striving for a goal, yet realize there will be many obstacles along the way. When failure occurs, they view it as momentary. They believe failure helps them to understand their abilities and provides them with added insight into errors or weaknesses. Failure allows healthy competitors to come to grips with their potential as well as to realize their inadequacies, both of which are crucial to the development of a realistic self-image. Failure enhances rather than destroys motivation for future competition if a competitor responds to it in this way.

Teaching the Process

As a parent, you can help your child learn this process through your words and actions. When your child fails and you respond with "What's wrong with you? You made so many errors it was ridiculous" or, "You're a complete failure. You're an embarrassment to the family," you are not teaching a healthy response to failure. If you say that failure is acceptable and a tool for growth but act otherwise when your child fails, your actions will speak louder than your words. The best way to respond to a child's competitive loss is to let the child know you love him or her and are proud of him or her for having tried. Then let your child say whatever he or she wants to say without offering judgment. Once the emotions that often come from disappointing losses have disappeared, you can raise thought-provoking questions: "What do you think of your performance today?" "Did you do what you wanted to do?" "Did you give it your best?" "What do you think you need to do better next time if you wish to improve?" "Do you need to modify what you are doing in practice?" These questions may be followed by reminders to your child that you can see improvement all the time, and that the good news in sport is that how he or she did today has nothing to do with tomorrow's performance unless he or she lets it.

Healthy and effective competitors are excited about striving for excellence. During the search, both winning and losing occur. Winning is a fantastically enjoyable experience, but winning is the dessert, not the main reason for competing.

Parents must strive to exhibit this attitude themselves when they compete, and not only in sports. They should use this approach in a wide variety of activities. Parents who have not been healthy competitors themselves can learn to view competition more rationally with their children.

Some healthy responses to failure for parents might include:

- Analyzing your performance after a defeat.
- Evaluating things both done well and done badly.
- Writing out a practice plan emphasizing drills to build on strengths and eliminate weaknesses.
- Sharing with other family members how much you enjoyed competing and telling them that even though you lost you learned a lot.
- Acknowledging the skill and positive attitude of the competitor who beat you.

You can also help your child understand the competitive process by seeking out others who are healthy competitors. When you observe healthy competitors with your child, praise their attitude toward competition. Point out the joy they appear to exude when they are competing. Speak in glowing terms of their enthusiastic response to other competitors. Note that whether they win or lose, they keep trying to improve. Emphasize it is the process of striving for excellence rather than the outcome that is most important.

The difficult part is for parents to explain and demonstrate to their child how this approach increases the possibility of success. A process orientation may sound great, but it wouldn't be valuable if it didn't lead to successful outcomes.

You need to help your child balance process and outcome. A useful strategy for doing so requires that your child understand and accept his or her abilities and limitations. Once these are fully accepted, the child can learn when to put greater emphasis on the process and when to move more in the direction of outcomes or product. The child can learn that the best way to improve the chances for a positive outcome is to improve upon the process or skills necessary for success.

Emphasize process over product when your child starts on a new endeavor, experiences failure in competition with others, or lacks ability, at least temporarily. Emphasizing striving will make these situations more enjoyable and productive, whereas emphasizing the result, at least at this time, will most likely destroy all interest in continued efforts. Don't allow the emphasis to shift to results if and when success begins to occur, because nothing is as pleasing as enjoying the process of improvement and getting successful results. This is an ultimate joy!

The key is first to turn your child on to the process. As positive results begin to appear, allow your child to enjoy the results while remembering the process that resulted in the improvement. This approach provides for optimal motivation for improvement of sport skills and will teach a strategy that can apply to future achievement tasks.

Let's face it; at some point in life, outcomes do matter. The teacher's students must learn; the salesperson must sell or starve; the engineer's bridge must be stable. A child who is only process oriented may never become a successful competitor. People such as gamblers or workaholics may get so lost in the process that they continue their activity even at the expense of mental, physical, and social well-being. Clearly, this isn't a desirable approach for your child.

On the other hand, a child may be so product oriented that goals such as prestige and money cause persistence even in the face of frustration or dislike for the activity. For a child athlete, the result might be, "I've been practicing baseball for 8 years, 3 hours a day, for that college scholarship. Now that I didn't get one, I'm quitting forever. I don't ever want to play this or any other sport again." As an adult the same individual might realize: "I've spent all of these years working for money and prestige. Now I have them and realize how foolish I've been. Money and prestige don't make me happy."

Too great or early an emphasis on the product is not good for your child. Your child needs to know and accept himself or herself to develop a healthy balance, even while striving to improve. A child who is afraid to fail or to identify strengths and weaknesses will never evolve into a healthy competitor. Testing is necessary if the child is to know where his or her strengths and weaknesses lie, information that can be gained only by focusing on the processes of sport.

The real challenge in sport is the competition itself. It doesn't matter who wins but who competes. In fact, competing and losing may be as valuable as competing and winning. The following poem by Ralph H. Coulson (1978) extols the virtues of the "second place finisher":

In Praise of Coming in Second

Whoever sings the praises of the almost winner, the second-best, the runner-up, the also ran. Names that make you think of a fellow who couldn't quite make it.

Don't let that fool you.

Ask the winner of any race how good a man is Mister Two. He'll tell you it's Mister Two who made him run so fast. Mister Two pressing hard at his heels, threatening always to overtake and pass him.

Ask the salesman who won the contest that kept him plugging after hours. Ask the director of the great corporation why they keep changing their product, seeking the added advantage.

What drives them? What keeps them hopping? It's Mister Two.

In this country, we're proud of the quality of our champions. Our big men come very big. Our fast men run very fast, and our great men are the greatest that a country could hope to be blessed with. And why is that?

Could it be because hot on the heels of every champion runs a Mister Two? . . . Mister Twos grow naturally in a land where the race is always open and everybody can run.

So this is for you, Mister Two. This is for all the days you tried for first and came in second. It's for the nights when you wonder if you ought to go on trying since nobody seems to notice.

We notice, Mister Two. We know the score. Winner or not, you're a natural champion. There couldn't be a race without you, Mister Two. (p. 12)

Follow these guidelines to teach your child the process of competitive success:

- Teach your child to have a goal and strive for the goal.
- Tell your child that winning isn't everything, nor is it unimportant.
- Teach your child to accept mistakes and failures as a necessary ingredient of success.
- Teach your child to view mistakes and failures as obstacles to be overcome.
- Encourage your child to take pride in giving his or her best.
- Teach your child that winning is the dessert, not the main course.
- Realize that you teach a great deal, intentionally or not, through role modeling. Children will usually try to do what they see their parents doing.
- Notice and reward your child for displaying behaviors consistent with good sportsmanship that show respect for other competitors.
- Tell your child that losing to a competitor only serves to improve his or her play.
- Teach your child to respect and appreciate other healthy competitors.

Winning Isn't a Dirty Word

Almost everyone values winning, but wanting to win at all costs is a problem. There is no doubt that winning is one of the objectives of sport, and while it is not the only one, it is the culminating and immediate measure of success.

Parents should not necessarily worry about coaches who emphasize winning, as long as winning is not the only thing these coaches care about. Unfortunately, the negatives associated with an overemphasis on winning have made some parents feel uncomfortable or self-conscious about advocating or even valuing winning.

A winning attitude is important, but it is sometimes confused with being overly critical or having a fear of losing. Adults who are emotionally upset by a loss or who create unnecessary pressure to win give winning a bad name. And even worse, such pressure may create children who fear failure so much they quit trying.

Your child can't be a great athlete without wanting to win. In order to be excellent, he or she must be willing to sacrifice, to work hard, to be dedicated to goals, and to strive for success. What is winning? One young swim coach told his swimmers:

> Real winning is clear to see. Winning is improving. Winning is learning. Winning is trying. Winning is the first time you are able to do a good flip turn in competition. Winning is finishing the race strong and well. Winning is performing better than you have ever performed at all before. Winning is listening and paying attention and applying what you hear from your coach. Winning is doing better every time. Winning is striving with all your might. Winning is never giving in to a feeling of being tired.
>
> Winning can happen to everybody! (Close, 1978, p. 12)

A Competitive Attitude

Parents, coaches, and scholars have argued for years about whether a child learns competitive desire or is born with it. There is still no clear-cut answer. Both influences play a role, with learning having the greater effect. Clearly, individual competitiveness varies. The variations are generally caused by different experiences. Parents, brothers, sisters, relatives, coaches, teammates, and an assortment of early cultural and social experiences will help determine the degree of competitiveness each child displays.

Developing the Desire to Be Competitive

How is the competitive desire developed? What are the behaviors teachers and parents can use to encourage the development of high levels of competitiveness in a child?

The desire to compete can be influenced as early as the age of 2 years. Parents who encourage their children to be independent and to do well at early ages tend to have children with higher levels of competitiveness. Mothers and fathers who reward self-reliance with affection and also insist on early observance of rules tend to have children who are more highly motivated and more independent.

Parents' general attitudes and personal needs have also been found to be predictive of their child-rearing practices. Parents' orientations toward achievement may influence their behavior toward their child. Parents who begin to allow and encourage independence in their child early are apt to be the ones for whom achievement is important. They reward their child for attempts to achieve and withdraw praise when the striving is missing. The earlier such love and affection are given, the greater the chance of developing an achievement-oriented child.

The achievement behavior of a child is directly related to the degree of positive reinforcement and recognition the mother and father give the child for his or her efforts. Typically, parents expect the same attitudes toward hard work and achievement in their child as they hold toward their own achievement. Unfortunately, this may mean that achieving parents will have negative attitudes toward a low-achieving child. When this happens, parents may try to do all they can to encourage achieving attitudes in their child but must be patient if the result does not occur immediately. High-achieving parents must be careful not to be too critical or pushy with their child.

Developing Achievement Motivation

To develop an achieving attitude in your child, you must assume a direct teaching role and set a good example. One of the most effective ways is to remember to reward the behaviors you wish to see repeated and to eliminate undesirable behaviors by withdrawing the rewards or reinforcements. Using love and affection to reinforce desired behaviors in your child is a powerful technique. You can help your child develop pride in his or her behavior with a mere hug or smile of approval. Similarly, the temporary withdrawal of love and affection can be a powerful cue to your child.

Your approval is a strong motivator that tells your child what you value.

Positive reinforcement is a strong influence on behavior. Your child will respond to the nice things you say and do by repeating whatever action caused your reward. When you say "thank you" for opening the door, or "nice try, I'm proud of you" when he or she tries something new, your child is more likely to attempt that behavior next time an opportunity to do so occurs. You must realize, however, that positive reinforcement must be carefully used, or your child will become dependent upon it. Your goal is to help your child learn to value hard work and achievement and be motivated to attain it. Self-motivation will be taught initially by rewarding desired behaviors and later by talking about how good it must have felt to accomplish the act. This sense of feeling good will then become a reinforcer itself, and you will no longer have to be present constantly to give rewards of affection or approval.

Your child needs to learn how to deal with frustrations and challenges that inevitably come with attempts to achieve as the first step toward direction and self-control. The child must learn that success is ultimately self-determined. Certainly, the child must know you will be there when he or she really needs you, but gradually must realize the important battles are fought alone. So when you provide an opportunity for independence and self-direction, and your child responds with an attempt in that direction, let praise flow!

You cannot overestimate the effect of the judicious use of praise and criticism. We know that in general, praise tends to raise levels of performance, but criticism tends to lower performance. Such evaluations also tend to affect your child's expectancy of success. If children are regularly praised for their efforts, they expect praise and will work for it—a good example of the self-fulfilling prophecy. Eventually, desire for praise will lead your child to enjoy persistent efforts and take pride in goal accomplishment, which will in turn lead to self-motivated behavior.

What if Motivation Is Missing?

Any time a child lacks a goal orientation or motivation, it is worth trying to understand why. The following are some of the more common reasons for a child to not have motivation.

Lack of Parental Role Model.   Many parents have difficulty teaching their children to be competitive because they do not provide a competitive role model themselves. A parent who has not been competitive or goal-oriented may not understand how to teach a child how to become a good loser. The child soon learns always to accept failure as an uncontrollable outcome. The child may have learned "There is nothing I can do, I always lose no matter how hard I try."

A parent who has been a poor competitor needs to better understand the process of competition to teach it to a child. You need not have been a competitor in sport, but you must understand and value the effort required to be successful. Otherwise, you may be overly sympathetic and allow your child to give up unnecessarily when faced with failure and frustration.

Pushed Too Hard.   Some parents are so concerned with raising a goal-oriented child that they push the child. In larger families the push may emphasize comparisons to brothers, sisters, or other relatives: "Why can't you be like your brother? Don't you even care? He has so much drive and you just sit around all day doing nothing. You'll never amount to anything. You're such an embarrassment to me."

Besides the negative impact of pushing, the use of such statements by parents might incite sibling rivalry that could last a lifetime. Comparisons made with other people, particularly those inside the family, may lead to jealousy, envy, and feelings of inadequacy. These responses, rather than enhancing goal directedness, will hinder the development of goal-seeking attitudes.

Feelings of Inadequacy.   Children will make comparisons whether or not parents emphasize competition. If one child is successful at many endeavors, it is not uncommon for other children in the family to feel inadequate. Some children increase their motivation and strive to live up to the family reputation when placed in this situation. Others avoid competitive situations. Many play it safe until they find a sure-win opportunity.

Children commonly respond to this situation by competing in totally different areas than their siblings. Often, even if parents are especially aware of the difficulties a child has in following in the footsteps of a talented brother or sister, pressure may come from teachers or coaches. Parents must be understanding and supportive of the child's search for a positive identity. Don't be afraid of talking with your child about his or her unique qualities and strengths.

An Only Child.   Today, many families have one child. This child may become the parents' only opportunity to prove they can be successful parents; as a result, they may teach the child to be a perfectionist. Anything short of perfection may be judged a failure. Soon the child's self-esteem is lowered, which results in either an anxious perfectionist or a child who avoids competition.

Another problem often faced by an only child is the absence of other children in the home to compete with on a regular basis. If other friends or surrogate siblings are not available, the child may have a hard time understanding how to compete with other children. Parents in this situation should be sure to invite other children to play or take the child places to play with others.

A Lack of Interest.   Sometimes a child doesn't seem to show interest or enthusiasm for any endeavor. Parents must be patient. They can serve as role models or provide opportunities and wait until the child shows an interest or a spark of enthusiasm. When this happens, supportive feedback may help. Sometimes parents will have to accept that a child doesn't like sport and hope that as an adult the child will develop an interest in some form of exercise or sport.

Should You Push Your Child?

The answer to this question is in some ways simple and in others complex. Most great athletes have not been pushed by their parents. Some who have reached the highest levels of sport have been provided with direction and encouragement, while others have been given a very strong push. In all these cases, *most* parents did what they did with the right intentions. They wanted to help their children, to get them started or give them a chance for success. Most also assumed their children would thank them for the push later, even if they didn't seem to appreciate it at the time.

Parents who push their children seem to fall into a consistent pattern of behaviors. They criticize the child for any sign of happiness following a loss. Even happiness following a less-than-perfect victory calls for alarm and a reprimand: "I'm amazed that you can feel satisfied with the way you performed today. I know you won, but you'll never be the best performing the way you did today." The child's standards are never good enough. Every time the child progresses and reaches one standard, the parent immediately resets the standard higher and holds back love and approval until it is met. This game often lasts a lifetime. The child slowly realizes that the parent's love is dependent upon performance and that the parent doesn't feel good about himself or herself unless the child is number one. As soon as the child is the best in the city, the rules change. Now the child must be best in the state; then love is only given for winning regionals, then nationals, then the world. And then it must be repeated again next year or there is no love or approval.

When withdrawal of love doesn't work, the pushy parent typically turns to more drastic measures. Privileges and rewards are given if the child practices hard enough; however, they are quickly taken away when efforts aren't judged good enough. Guilt, fear, and hatred of other competitors are regularly used as quick and easy sources of motivation.

Parents who use this approach put their children in a precarious position. If children accept this approach, they only allow themselves the luxury of feeling good about themselves if they win. Fear of failure becomes a primary motivator. If they reject this approach, they must separate themselves from their parents, learn to think for themselves, and try to love and accept themselves regardless of their successes, failures, or ranking. Doing this is difficult even for adult athletes, let alone for young ones. Some children, however, have been able to achieve this as they mature.

We spoke with a great professional athlete who had been continually pushed and was unhappy despite unmatched success. She told us that even when she was 29 her father was visibly upset and unhappy any time she did not win. Whenever she played in out-of-town competition and called home after competing, her father would not speak to her unless she had triumphed. Eventually this athlete concluded that

> I love my dad because he is my father, but I don't like him as a person. I do not want to be like him or feel like him. And I would never, ever do to a child what he did to me. I've been number one in the world in my sport, and it is not even close to being worth it. Why destroy feelings of self-respect and self-worth and a parent's relationship with a child just to be a success?

Pushing a child is a strategy that appears to work in the short run, but is total disaster in the long run. Eventually it emotionally destroys the child, wastes his or her talent, and wipes out what could have been a great relationship. The child never feels comfortable because the parent is always standing by, ready to judge whether the child tried hard enough or measured up. The pushed child is never allowed the freedom to attain internal peace and happiness.

To us, it is crystal clear that the athletes who have become the happiest, healthiest, most successful, and most capable of sustaining motivation throughout their lives have been those who either never were pushed or, if they were pushed in their childhood years, were given the freedom to choose their level of involvement by their teens. This latter point is absolutely essential. Teenagers who are not given the freedom to choose where they spend their time and energy will invariably feel forced to practice and play. They will hate every day of it and feel as if they must play in order to make their parents happy. The sad reality is that a number of young athletes who probably would love sport if they were given the freedom to choose end up hating it because playing was not their decision. Any parent who is not willing to let a child decide to quit or continue by the teen years has made sport far too important.

Developing Mental Toughness

Most parents seem to know that effective competitors are mentally tough. What is mental toughness? Can it be developed or is a child born with it?

The first step to developing mental toughness is to admit the inherent frailty of being human. You will make mistakes; you will fail; you are not perfect. The second step is to learn to view those mistakes or failures as opportunities to learn about yourself and improve. The third step is to learn to take pride in knowing that no matter how difficult a competition may be, you will give it your best shot. "Hanging in there" is a highly valued trait.

Your child can learn these attitudes only if you provide praise and encouragement. Encouragement will rob failure of its sting and allow your child to keep his or her head up, stay motivated, and keep trying even when everything seems to be going wrong.

When your child has been playing poorly, it may be helpful to talk about a time in your life when everything appeared to be going badly. Relate how perseverance paid off because you believed in yourself. Or actively look in newspapers and magazines for an article about an athlete who overcame a great obstacle, such as repeated failure, to become successful. In other words, search for an indirect way to encourage your child to be mentally tough.

When your child follows your advice, let him or her know how much you and others admire such toughness and persistence. Remind your child of the fact that this attitude makes him or her special because most people quit when faced with such difficulties. Emphasize that you are proud of your child because you know that with this attitude success will certainly follow. Do not say you are proud because the child did what you said to do! Let your child enjoy the fact that he or she decided to "hang in there."

Self-Confidence

Despite the virtues of mental toughness, children cannot persist and attain goals if they are always setting themselves up for failure. No one is that tough. Make sure your child is being honest about his or her level of ability. Help your child identify activities in which he or she can be successful. Initial successes do not have to come from sport-related activities. Any endeavor that can lead to a successful accomplishment can be a step in the right direction.

Choosing the Right Activity

As mentioned previously, your child may be attracted to a sport that is popular among other children in your community. If your child is talented, such a sport may be ideal. Incentives for increased motivation, hard practice, and the resulting success will be plentiful.

Even if your child isn't highly successful, it may be best to allow the child to remain involved in the popular activity if he or she is happy. Your child will enjoy the friendships made from that activity. Remember, however, that sometimes simply becoming a part of the team or the "in group" becomes so valued that the child learns little about personal achievement. A child involved in a team activity in which he or she lacks talent will learn that trying hard and persisting are not valued and may feel athletes with talent will play more no matter how hard he or she tries to improve. If this situation is not managed properly, such experiences can be negative for your child.

Martie, a young child who was a member of the local junior high basketball team, came home from practice quite discouraged and said:

> Basketball is so unfair. I've been practicing for 2 years now and I can't even get to play. I was hoping to be a starter this year. I was actually starting for a week. Then coach talked Terry into playing. Terry has always played soccer, but never basketball. The first day at practice Terry starts before me. What good does it do to practice? I don't want to eat. I'm going up to my room.

Martie's example shows why it is useful to emphasize the process of striving for success in sport, and not just the product. Martie must understand that making it in sport is not easy; nothing worth attaining ever is. To make it in sport, Martie must be taught the importance of hanging in there, remaining confident, and increasing intensity in practice. Martie must know that getting discouraged will only make the problem worse and will be viewed as a sign of weakness by the coach.

If your child repeats this scene on a regular basis, chances are he or she is in the wrong sport, or at the wrong level of competition, or merely a "late bloomer." You may need to talk to your child about reality, even if he or she doesn't want to hear it at the time. You may begin by helping your child realize that sport, like the rest of life, is not always fair. This is particularly true in team sports, where the coach holds a great amount of power and control over your child's success. As an example, list your child's positive features relative to other children. Your child may be more intelligent, better looking, or more personable than many other classmates. Point out that this isn't fair either. Everyone has certain strengths and weaknesses, some capable of being changed, some not. A child must learn to put energy into the areas that he or she can change rather than worrying about the ones that cannot be changed.

When helping your child deal with this problem, remind the young athlete that he or she may be a late bloomer. The skills the child develops through patient practice will pay off with successful performance when the body matures.

If your child refuses to accept these points, you might suggest that he or she could be in the wrong activity relative to his or her present talents. Ask your child to describe his or her strengths. Help the child determine another activity to try.

Once your child decides upon a new activity, don't allow the child to look at the past as a wasted experience. Remind the child that a lot was learned from the experience that could help him or her in the future. Perhaps most importantly, your child has learned about his or her strengths and weaknesses. The child has learned to be honest with himself or herself and to realize the importance of this in attaining success and happiness.

Ralph Sampson, the 1980 and 1981 College Basketball Player of the Year for the University of Virginia, told us:

> I tried lots of other activities before I found I had talent at basketball. My dad was a musician and I tried learning how to play at least four different instruments before I ever tried and found some success at basketball. It sure was a nice feeling to discover an activity in which I had talent.

Helping Your Child Avoid Repeated Failure

"A child grows from failure." "There is great strength in learning from failure." These statements sound wonderful and contain some truth, but constant or repeated failure is not necessarily beneficial either to psychological growth or to progress toward more concrete goals. Constant failure may mean you have overemphasized the importance of persistence and overcoming obstacles. While these are valuable and often useful attitudes to learn, they may actually prevent growth and realistic adjustment if taken to extremes.

Repeated failure is caused sometimes by factors that can be modified, such as practice quality or intensity. Other times it is caused by competing at too advanced a level of competition so that failure is almost guaranteed, even with an efficient plan for improvement.

Help your child learn to evaluate failures honestly and accurately. Without a regular evaluation of the direction and quality of effort, of the ability available, and of the difficulty of the challenge, including the quality of the opposition, a child may get lost in a self-defeating cycle of repeated failure. Everyone needs success as well as the ability to understand and deal with defeat or lack of success. Children must realize they are not failures just because they are not always judged to be successful.

Your child must realize there is no way to guarantee winning at sport. Anyone who has ever competed has lost. No one can escape it, including your child. Your child won't have to accept it on a regular basis, but he or she must be capable of experiencing it. Your child also will not compete alone. Some people will help your child win; others will try to undermine him or her and help your child fail.

In order to attain goals, children must decide who they are, what they want, and what they stand for in life. They must learn who their friends are and who wants to get in their way. They must learn to believe in themselves, but also learn to listen to friends.

You and your child will become close friends because of the many emotional struggles you will share. You will learn from each other. There is no way you or your child will be failures. If you have increased the likelihood that your child will be happy and healthy, you will be successes.

Building Your Child's Confidence

You can't be mentally tough if you're not self-confident. Confidence is crucial to happiness and success—yet it is so elusive. You must encourage children in a way that constantly makes them feel good about their abilities, their personalities, and their bodies if you want them to have self-confidence. It is especially important to strive to make your child feel good about characteristics that are unchangeable. At the same time, it is important to instill the desire to change qualities that need to be changed and that are changeable. Convince a child who has not found success by age 10 that, with dedication and persistence, he or she can be successful by age 15. Help your child feel proud because he or she is more willing than others to practice and concentrate for long periods of time. These efforts will eventually pay off in improvement.

Developing a belief in the value of persistent effort may be the key to eventual happiness in life as well as in sport. Helping your child develop a belief in persistent effort will probably simultaneously help develop self-confidence and further increase your child's desire to be a winner.

If you are like many parents, you might find yourself making statements like "I was never a good athlete. I was too small and too weak. I was frustrated despite trying hard. I never made the team." Maybe you are thinking there is no sense in even encouraging your child, because it will only cause frustration. If you find yourself harboring such thoughts, remember many great athletes had parents who were not gifted participants. Many great athletes began by dreaming of greatness and then setting down goals.

When Olympic decathlon champion Bruce Jenner was in high school, there were always runners who performed much better than he did. He reports he never let this discourage him, but rather established a realistic goal of becoming the best at performing many sports instead of just one. For Bruce Jenner, this approach was certainly effective, but many children need to realize they can't be great at everything but perhaps can be the best at something. Other children may learn they can't be truly great at anything, but they can always give their best. Often this is the most admirable, if not the most rewarded, of abilities.

When Jean Claude Killy was 13 years old, he wrote his dream down on paper. His goal was to win three gold medals in snow skiing. His friends said his goal was impossible, but Killy has since proved them wrong. Parents can help their child greatly in life if they help change "I can't" to "I can," or at least "I'll try my best." Help your child realize that happiness, friendship, and joy in sport can be realized much more quickly if hard work coexists with faith in oneself.

Dr. Craig Fisher (1982), a sport psychologist working with children, has studied the development of self-confidence. He suggests that if you wish to instill self-confidence in your child, you should remember these 15 points:

1. When compliments are paid to your child, don't make them too "sugary" or too manipulative. They should be sincere and straightforward.
2. Teach your child the importance of accepting praise without reservation and embarrassment.
3. Appreciative praise is stronger than evaluative praise. For example, you could say, "I get psyched watching you play," as opposed to, "You're a great ball player."
4. Athletes should be convinced that success is moving towards goals, rather than just attaining them. The process is very important in building self-confidence.

5. It is both okay and beneficial for a young athlete to bask in the limelight of success. Allow your child to be proud of his accomplishments.
6. Provide praise when your child displays a positive and enthusiastic attitude.
7. Go out of your way to look for opportunities to reward and praise your child when he does something correctly.
8. Correct your child in a manner that is both positive and constructive.
9. Acknowledge the fact that errors are part of sport and that they can be used as cues to enhance future performance.
10. Do not use sarcasm and "put downs" as your major interactive style of communication.
11. Do not withhold rewarding your child. Waiting for the ultimate expression of excellence may take a lifetime.
12. Do not publicly criticize your child unless there are no alternatives.
13. Do not give your child too much to learn or too many directions at any one point in time.
14. Do not hinder creativity by overcontrolling the environment and demanding that everything be done the way you say.
15. Do not lose emotional control. If you do, you will be teaching your child to do the same.

Self-Discipline

Personal discipline is a key ingredient in sport success. Andrea Jaeger, the tennis player, has attributed her disciplined attitude to her European background and her father's influence in encouraging her to practice. Similarly, Bjorn Borg has often mentioned the strong influence of his parents, who had repeatedly told him to control his temper or they would take away his racket. After one racket throwing incident, he was denied tennis for over a month, and as a result quickly learned to discipline himself.

The discipline to persist is important to success at most endeavors in life, but even the most motivated and disciplined young athlete occasionally questions his or her motivation. Recognize that your child will have to make a decision each time this happens. If your child truly loves the activity, the result will be an affirmation of continued commitment. Your child will maintain and increase self-discipline through this process. Children must be helped to understand that no one can compete for them and that they must make the commitment to practice and improve. The parent's job is to be there, to act as a sounding board, and to provide support for demonstrated self-discipline.

There is no way a child will survive in sport without self-discipline and the willingness to be disciplined by others. As parents, you must make sure to discuss and reach agreement upon the rules of behavior for your child. You must also agree upon who will enforce the rules, how they will be enforced, and when they will be enforced. Disagreement about dealing with your child must occur behind closed doors.

Disciplined behavior will only occur if rewards and punishment are used consistently. Parents who vacillate confuse their child. This means you must have rules of behavior that you believe in and are committed to if you are going to be consistent. Although you can most effectively teach discipline by behaving consistently, no parent can be perfect. When you err, you can strive to improve and learn from your mistakes.

Time Management

An individual who is going to be an athlete will be forced to learn how to manage time effectively, especially if success in school is to be coupled with fun and success in sport. A child who does not manage time well probably procrastinates and will fail in one or both areas. Unless your child is especially gifted, he or she cannot possibly give equal attention to every activity. There are too many exciting things to do in today's world, and your child will have to learn to set priorities and make choices.

A child has many attractive activities available: music lessons, acting, newspaper experience, debate team, scouting, volunteer activities. The list could go on and on. More than likely, your child will not be able to participate in all the attractive, available activities. Sooner or later the scout leader will say, "You can't go for your next merit badge if you don't make the trip this weekend. Are you going to be a scout or a basketball player?" Eventually the music instructor may ask, "Are you going to commit yourself to music or sport? I have many talented students, and if you are not willing to put more time into practicing and recitals, I can't waste my valuable time with you." Choosing between two options is not always easy or desirable, but the necessity of making a decision appears to be a reality in today's specialized society. Such decisions will force a child to set priorities, to evaluate strengths and weaknesses.

Parents can help in making these decisions, but it must ultimately be the child's choice.

Once a child chooses certain activities, he or she needs to learn the importance of setting a specific schedule to follow. Failure to plan and organize time may lead to rushed, sloppy, or incomplete efforts. It may also lead to procrastination—"I'll do it first thing Sunday night." A child needs to learn the importance of assigning a specific time to a task. If a particularly large project, such as a term paper, needs to be done, breaking it into a series of smaller tasks is often a valuable aid. The same is true for sport. Help the child to plan ahead, to set goals, because failing to plan is planning to fail!

If possible, estimate the time required to complete each activity or task, then add 5 or 10 minutes to every hour because most people underestimate the time needed. Some children need to do their time management in writing to commit themselves to their schedules. Others can effectively manage time in their heads. Don't mandate that everything be done in writing unless you think it is necessary.

Routines

Most children respond well to routines. Having a schedule can be useful, particularly in controlling stress, because the threat of the unknown is one of the major causes of childhood fear. Family routines such as "first we eat, then we do the dishes, then we practice our sports," set the ground rules.

An established routine can also aid in opening communication. Many parents find it helpful to set aside a certain period of time each day to be available to the child. Even a 15-minute segment will make a difference. Let your child know that you are there to talk, play catch, or listen. Let the child know you have set aside time even if he or she doesn't want to use it.

Procrastination

Many young athletes are procrastinators. They seem to avoid doing some tasks, especially homework and housework. Such procrastination results when they have too many things to do, but have no clear priorities or goals. For example:

Sally really wanted to make the basketball team. Her goals were to be well liked, to contribute to the team, and to play well. Her Achilles heel was her desire to get involved with more and more fringe activities. She volunteered to manage the equipment, offered to come early and check on uniforms, agreed to keep the ongoing statistics, and even agreed to wash the towels. She had many things to do but little time to practice, and she worried about not getting everything done. As she worried, she avoided tackling her responsibilities. A vicious cycle developed.

How can we help Sally avoid this problem? The first key would be to help her learn not to volunteer for everything, to learn to say no, and to place priorities on some of her activities. Once she establishes a set of responsibilities, she should use the goal-setting techniques previously discussed. She will feel a sense of pride as she accomplishes small goals and will also develop the momentum to continue working.

What's the cure for procrastination? It's JDD—just do it, darn it. Unfortunately, for most youngsters, the solution isn't that easy. However, there are some steps and guidelines that will help your children accomplish tasks.

- *Break down a task into smaller goals.* Setting the goal of learning to dribble the basketball behind the back, then the reverse dribble, and finally the between-the-legs dribble is much easier than trying to learn all three dribbles at once. Small steps, with small goals, do not seem so impossible, unmanageable, or overwhelming.
- *Choose a starting point that is pleasant and realistic.* Not all tasks are fun, but most have some less unpleasant aspects. Start there. Early success will help motivate a child toward continued effort.
- *Don't waste too much time preparing or worrying.* It is amazing how much time can be spent preparing to start. In Sally's case, she took forever to sharpen her pencils, clear her desk, get a soft drink, and adjust her stereo before she could even start to work on the team statistics. She needs to learn to tackle the project head on.
- *Pick a special time.* Choose a time to work on each project. You may decide the child should do all the "maintenance projects" first, such as taking out the garbage and sharpening pencils. Then set a time for homework. Should the child practice sport first and then study, or vice versa? During summers or free days, decide on the best time of day for each activity.
- *Set a schedule and reward accomplishments.* Everyone works more effectively with an incentive. You may help by deciding what needs to be done and providing a reward for each task completed. For example, if Sally likes to shoot baskets, set up a system in which she can earn free time to shoot baskets by completing some specific tasks.

Values

Values in the sport world have changed rapidly in recent years. Many parents, although wanting their children to take part in sport, are afraid their offspring will be taught values inconsistent with their own.

For the most part, values are taught to your children by authority figures or by those who have power over their lives. For example, someone who says, 'If I ever see you cheat again while playing, you won't play for 2 weeks," is emphasizing a value. Unfortunately, just saying it is not enough. Actions are far more crucial. If you tell your child not to cheat in sport, and yet your child watches you cheat when you play, you will probably teach your child that cheating is really okay (at least if you are an adult, or if your dad isn't watching!).

Most parents who have been successful at teaching values to their children are firm and are able to express displeasure openly. Such expressions of disappointment or displeasure must be done with emotional control and with love. You should try to explain why the value is so important and put an arm around your child as you are discussing it. Then explain that you are displeased because you care so much about his or her health and happiness.

During your child's adolescent years, you may feel life is a constant battle over values. Your child at this age is seeking independence and is no longer afraid to question your power or values. A child who must live totally by his or her parents' values cannot be independent. Your child at this age will want to establish and live by his or her own set of values.

In the process of forming values, your child may seek out inconsistencies between the values you have been teaching and the way you have acted in the past and may throw examples of such inconsistencies in your face, especially during an argument. You must remember not to take such attacks personally. In fact, you should try to enjoy them because they are the seeds that lead to the development of values. Understand, however, that you must also show discipline and restraint.

If you are a parent who has not developed a commitment and belief in the values you teach, this is a good time to question your own values. Perhaps you will find you really are committed to your values, or maybe you will find your values are outdated and inappropriate. By displaying a willingness to listen and reconsider, you show your child the value of continually reappraising personal values. Remember that ultimately your child will develop and live with his or her own values throughout life. As a parent your responsibility is to help guide your child in the development of these values.

Coaches' Values

Children mimic almost everyone who is important to them. The coach is one of the most important persons in the world of young athletes, which may present a wonderful advantage if the coach has the same values as your family. Mimicry may be a problem when your child's coach teaches moral judgments that may not match yours, however. For example, a coach may encourage players to break or push the rules to the limit as long as they don't get caught. Your child's coach may scream at the umpire over a close call and thus teach your child that the "end justifies the means"—particularly if the next call goes his or her way. As the parent, it is your job to educate your child as to the appropriate behavior. This is not an easy task!

Children often learn accidentally by pairing different behaviors with reinforcers. For example, a friend tells of a baseball game in which a young child was batting. Pat stood in the batter's box and took three strikes without even swinging. On strike three, the coach yelled, "What's the matter with you, don't you even care?" Pat ran back to the dugout to sit dejectedly and watch the other batters. The next hitter had a similar problem. He let the first pitch go by, and then swung wildly at the next two for three strikes. He immediately threw off his helmet and slammed down the bat! The coach responded by saying, "That's okay. Nice try, next time you'll get 'em!" The next time Pat was up, he let the first strike go by but swung wildly at the next two, threw down his helmet and bat, and was rewarded for his actions when the coach said, "Much better, you'll get a hit next time!"

What did Pat learn? He learned that it is apparently okay to strike out as long as you get mad and throw down your helmet! This example shows that you need to determine carefully what behaviors you wish to reinforce.

Parents have every reason to be concerned with the values of other adults who teach their child. The coach will be very influential in your child's life. You should take time to talk with your child's coach about his or her moral values. Are they consistent or inconsistent with yours? Only then can you decide if you want your child to play for a certain coach. Only then can you be aware that a coach is teaching different values and that you must discuss how to cope with this different orientation.

A coach whose values do not agree with yours may provide a perfect opportunity for you to help your child deal with differences of attitude and opinion. If you have reared your child with love and have lived by the values you have preached, the child is likely to accept your values in the long run. But be careful not to leave it to chance. You must watch carefully, discuss openly, and be ready to see your child test other ideas and actions.

At a recent basketball game, for example, a young player was accidentally hit in the head under the basket. Not knowing who fouled him, Chris retaliated by tripping the next player who came down the court. As a result Chris was ejected from the game. The coach had several options in this situation. If the coach punished Chris merely by benching him in the next game, Chris may learn only that he should not trip others when the coach or official is watching and may miss the point that intentionally tripping or hurting another person is wrong. It is important for coaches to discuss the behavior and be sure the child understands why the behavior is inappropriate. If the coach does not do so, the parents must!

Sportsmanship

Let's pursue this example a bit further. The player, Chris, must understand the difference in intent. The opponent accidentally hit him, whereas Chris's behavior was deliberate. The understanding of intent is critical to establishing mature moral reasoning. Children under 8 years old often cannot understand the concept of intent because they are unable to put themselves in another person's place and feel the consequences. In this conformity phase, children play by the rules or else; however, as they become more mature, they will need to understand why they should do certain things to develop a sense of right and wrong. This is a prime time to discuss children's actions and help them develop their own moral reasoning.

Indicating approval for desired behavior or disapproval for inappropriate actions is important to fostering good sportsmanship. Love and positive reinforcement will help focus a child's attention on good behavior. Punishment for undesirable behavior must be followed by an explanation of why the behavior was wrong and a description of appropriate behavior. Reasoning and explanation allow a child to associate behavior with rewards or punishments.

Phrases such as "I am disappointed in you because . . ." or "It makes me unhappy when you . . ." help the child to understand your position.

During the early childhood years, it is important for parents to respond consistently. If you let your child trip someone at home but issue a reprimand for tripping during organized games, he or she may think tripping is bad in basketball but okay at other times. You must help the child understand the reasons for good behavior. Communication is the key.

Interacting With Officials

Sportsmanship is an important concept to teach. Because we know that children also learn by imitation, your child must see you as a good sport, someone who treats officials and coaches with respect.

Children must learn to accept an official's call, even if they disagree with it. They need to know officials are human and can be wrong, but in the end officials do the best job they can. Your child should understand the role and function of officials. If the young athlete recognizes that the striped-shirted individual is there to help make the game more enjoyable by keeping it safe and fair, he or she will be much more likely to respect and help the official. You may want to let your child try to officiate a game, an experience that is likely to help him or her understand and appreciate officials. The child will begin to understand that an official has a difficult job and can honestly miss a call, a first step in a child's learning to accept the official's calls regardless of whether he or she agrees.

Discussing the officiating in a game after it is over may be important. You and your child should recognize if an official has been inconsistent in judgments or interpretation of the rules. Such inconsistencies affect the game, but should not serve as an excuse for losing or reduce the pleasure of victory. The discussion should be held to learn for the future, not to rehash the past.

Summary

Helping your child be a successful athlete involves not only providing for the development of foundational skills, but also facilitating the development of the basic elements of a positive self-concept and value system related to the sport.

Successful athletes have learned to deal with failure and use it to direct action. Children must learn to view mistakes and failures merely as obstacles to be overcome. It is important for children to develop the attitude that disappointments are all right because they make the joys and successes that much better.

There may be many reasons some children lack motivation, but several seem directly related to the parents' influence. In particular, children who lack role models, are pushed too hard, or develop a feeling of inadequacy may lose their interest in sport.

In contrast, the mental toughness and self-discipline needed for success in sport can be developed through supportive and successful experiences. Such experiences help children become self-directed and confident as they enjoy the struggle for success.

The importance of adult role models in teaching moral values cannot be overemphasized. Most of us learn by what we see and experience. You must be a reinforcer of desired behaviors as well as a living example of those behaviors.

Section II

Guiding Your Child's Early Sport Experience

Parents play an important role in the sport experience of their children. You may provide the strongest influence, either as a direct role model through personal participation or as someone who guides and encourages development. Such guidance will not always be easy. There will be disagreements, disappointments, and sometimes even tears.

One of the most important relationships you will have that will affect your child's progress in sport is your relationship with your child's coach. You will have to learn to communicate effectively with your child's coach so you can guide your child's progress without interfering unnecessarily. You also will need to know how to handle conflicts between your child and his or her coach. Finally, you should try to find the best possible coach for your child.

Both parents and coaches run into sensitive issues in sport. It's often hard to know when to encourage a child to be confident and assertive or when a child has become overconfident or too aggressive. It's also difficult to know how to talk with a child about sport performance in a way that encourages without being pushy or overcritical. You will need to learn your child's verbal and nonverbal clues to know how he or she feels if you want to communicate the right ideas at the right times.

You may feel that you could be the best coach for your child. You may be right, but there are many pitfalls in coaching your own child, and we have listed the possible problems so you can consider them before making a choice. There are also some special problems for the children of professional athletes.

Whether you decide to coach on your own or simply want to help your child progress, knowing some techniques for practice will help you. We'll give you some keys to making practice motivating and useful. We'll also mention some effective techniques to use during practice sessions.

If you are going to assist your child in practice, it is important that you be able to understand and analyze skills. Learning six basic principles of movement will allow you to look at any sport skill and make suggestions for improvement.

Two final areas of interest you should have in your child's sport career are injury prevention and nutrition. With proper training and basic safety precautions, athletes can avoid most injuries. You should also be aware of the special hazards strenuous activity can have for growing children. Some basic information about nutrition should be all you need to keep your child athlete eating right. We'll talk briefly about food supplements and discuss some questions that frequently arise regarding eating and competition. The topic of weight loss is also often important to athletes, and we'll talk about sensible and not-so-sensible ways for them to lose weight.

Parents Working With Coaches

Chapter 6

A child who is to grow into a successful athlete will need a good coach, one who enjoys developing the child. Parents must constantly strive to say and do things that foster the development of a *positive* and *trusting* relationship between the coach and their young athlete. Parents who accidentally or intentionally cause friction between coach and athlete will likely hinder their child's athletic development. We cannot overstate this point. Coaches hold tremendous power in sport. They pull the strings of success and control who plays and who doesn't.

Many times coach-parent problems occur when coaches' goals and values are different from parents'. Parents must realize that the more they are committed to certain beliefs, the more hesitant they will be to accept information that threatens those beliefs. When parents and coaches both have strongly held beliefs that are the same, everything is fine. When their beliefs differ, however, there may be increased conflicts. The more involved parents are with their child's sport life, the greater the likelihood of intense feelings and potential conflicts with a coach.

When such conflicts arise, something must be done. Parents can try to change a coach to their way of thinking, either through calm, logical reasoning or through emotionally charged moral arguments —but coaches will usually become defensive when parents become emotional and the attempt will fail. Instead, parents should try to avoid thinking that the coach's views are right or wrong, good or bad. Such thinking leaves no middle ground.

Coaches believe they know what is best for your child as a person and as an athlete, so trust your child's coach and remain receptive to his or her ideas and flexible in your ability to adjust to them.

Interacting With a Coach

Sooner or later, parents of every young athlete will interact with their child's coach. These opportunities may be pleasant and friendly or unpleasant and filled with bitterness. Unless your child is a gifted athlete, the quality of your conversations with your child's coach may greatly influence your child's success.

When You and the Coach Have Different Expectations

Nothing feeds the fire of discord like a coach who has low expectations for a child when the parents have high expectations. The coach may believe the child has little or no talent, whereas the parents feel the child has unlimited ability. Given this situation, many parents feel the coach has judged their child prematurely. They may believe the coach dislikes their child or is out to get him or her. In their minds, their child is not getting a fair chance.

Far too often, parents become emotional and defensive in such a situation, a response that will almost always lead the coach to become increasingly alienated from the child. Such a result may be particularly likely for the coach of a youth sport, who is coaching your child and many others for little or no salary and is trying to do what is best for each child. By reacting emotionally, parents may subtly sabotage their child's chances for success.

You must be careful not to let your love for your child cause you to jump to faulty conclusions. If you do, the outcome will be fairly predictable: You will not be satisfied with your child's progress.

Some parents become blind to their child's weaknesses. As a result, they see only the positive aspects of their child's contribution and are unwilling to accept their child as being anything but exceptionally talented. To these parents, the grass is always greener elsewhere. Other coaches seem better or more qualified, and the program never seems to be run as well as they would like.

Parents experiencing all or some of these feelings must attempt to evaluate honestly their feelings, their child, and the coach. As a parent, ask yourself what you can do to improve the situation. Do what you can to make the sport experience more positive for your child. If you still feel the coach or the program is failing your child, bring it to the coach's attention in a nonthreatening manner. Often the coach will thank you for the information or even agree with you. If so, let the coach know you are concerned and that you are willing to help. Strive to be part of the solution rather than part of the problem.

When You Are Publicly Critical of the Coach

When young athletes experience sport-related problems, it is all too common for parents to criticize the coach publicly. The following comment from a parent is a good example:

> We're really disgusted. Our child is really interested and excited about playing and improving. This darn program is so crummy we can't believe it. There is no way anyone can get good in this program. Coach doesn't seem to care about the program. He probably doesn't even know what he's doing. Heck, our child is talented and is just being wasted.

Parents with this view receive far more than their fair share of the coach's time, attention, and energy. But what is the value of this attitude for their child? Or for the program?

Publicly critical parents seldom complain directly to the coach, but they do complain to each other, to parents of other athletes (especially unhappy ones), and to their child. Such parents seem to take pleasure in putting coaches down. On the surface, their thoughts and complaints might seem logical, but parents who understand the coach's viewpoint and are aware that the coach has many other children to teach find the complaints irrational. Regardless, complaints of critical parents are wasted on those powerless to explain behaviors or institute change. Only direct discussion with the coach offers the possibility of understanding or resolving the complaints.

Unfortunately, a child living in a home where the parents are critical of the coach has a choice to make: Either shut out the parents' thoughts or begin to lose faith in the coach. The latter choice will prevent the child from accepting the coach, believing in the coach's approach, and adjusting to it. The former choice is an obvious negative one for the family. The child will be the loser either way.

Parents who find themselves in this situation may believe family authority is the ultimate authority. They feel they know more about helping their child than the coach does and therefore are the only ones who know how to work with their child. However, parents must allow themselves to trust their child's coach. If an honest analysis convinces them it is impossible to trust the coach, they must find another coach. If they continue to complain and criticize in public, they will only guarantee problems for their child.

When the Coach Brings Up Problems

Although some parents become too critical of their child's coach, other parents have a different problem: They don't take the time to find out how the child is doing. Many parents don't have much time because they're busy trying to earn a living and often blame the coach when their child has a problem. If you find yourself in this situation, perhaps you are to blame. When the coach comes to speak with you in an effort to understand your child's problem and you respond as though the coach is prying, chances are you are feeling guilty. Maybe you feel guilty because you give little time or thought to your child. Perhaps your guilt is due to uncertainty or family unhappiness. Whatever you are feeling, keep your composure when you are talking to the coach. Be grateful your child has a coach who cares enough to come to you. It would certainly be easier for the coach to avoid the issue and to skip the discussion with you! Be appreciative that the coach is looking out for your child. You may have become so preoccupied with your own problems that you were not aware your child was experiencing difficulties.

Parents undergoing marital conflict often think their child is oblivious to the problem. Not only is this incorrect, but family conflicts may be a greater concern to a child than to the parents. Rather than blame the coach for prying, parents must be willing to listen to the coach, accept his or her thoughts on the child's difficulties, and be thankful for the insight. This is a good time to ask the coach for continued interest and understanding of the child and the family situation.

When You Want to Express Your Concerns

The emotionally charged nature of sport, the public attention given to athletes, and the parents' and child's love of sport make it easy for parents to react emotionally and irrationally when they are unhappy with their child's progress.

For example, Coach Jones was about to call Jenna's father to talk to him about Jenna's frequent absences from practice. She wanted to tell him about how talented Jenna is and that if she would just come to practice, Jenna would be starting and developing into an outstanding player.

But before she could call, Coach Jones bumped into Jenna's dad in the grocery store. He confronted her angrily, demanding to know why Jenna wasn't starting. Before Coach Jones could explain, the father, seething with anger, suggested that a female coach couldn't possibly know much about basketball or judging talent.

By this time, Coach Jones was very upset by the father's belligerent attitude and statements and by the fact that this unplanned meeting was making her late on her one free evening this week. Coach Jones finally said: "Perhaps if you had taught your child how to be responsible and saw to it that she went to practice, I could coach her."

There is little doubt that Coach Jones' response was understandable. But it was unfortunate, because encounters such as this almost always lead to increased hostility and defensiveness. Eventually, the relationship may deteriorate until it can't be salvaged. More importantly, such an encounter will likely strain the already tenuous relationship between coach and athlete.

Parents must try to evaluate situations objectively so their responses will not be emotional or irrational. It is usually not the event or situation by itself that causes the hostile reaction; it is the individuals' negative perception of the situation.

You must place your child ahead of your desire to let your emotions flow. You must be free of emotionally charged reactions when you write to or talk with the coach, even though it may be easier to ridicule, attack, or speak in an annoying tone of voice.

Remember the following points when you feel emotionally upset about the coach's actions:

- An emotional reaction or attack on your child's coach seldom helps your child; in fact, it often results in harm.
- Always trust that your child's coach is looking out for your child's best interest until it is proven otherwise.
- The chances of teaching your child how to respond effectively

to his or her coach are far greater than the chances of changing the coach.

• At the first thought of concern over your child's treatment by a coach, take the initiative. Talk with the coach and ask "What is my child failing to do?" or "What can my child do to improve his or her standing?"

If you must talk to your child's coach about a problem, learn to walk the fine line between assertiveness and hostile aggressiveness. An assertive approach does not put the coach down but does allow you to clearly express your feelings.

For example, Jenna's father could have said, "Hello, Coach Jones, am I ever glad to see you. I know this isn't the best time to talk, but there is something I need to discuss with you. Is there a good time for me to call you or come and see you?" or, "Coach Jones! Hi, I'm Jenna's father. Glad to see the team is going well. I am, however, really concerned over Jenna's attitude and her performance. Do you have a few moments now, or could I meet with you sometime soon?"

When you are talking with a coach about an issue regarding your child, you should state your true feelings, stay calm, and listen attentively to the coach's reply. Try to remember that, like parents, coaches also experience stress. Realize that you are both more likely to respond in a defensive, emotional manner if either of you is upset. Keeping this important point in mind will allow you to have a better chance of helping rather than hindering your child if you decide it is time to intervene.

Responding to Coach-Athlete Frustrations

Anyone who takes part in sport experiences failure, disappointment, and frustration, but learning to deal with such situations and the resulting feelings is actually one of the true benefits of sport.

Imagine your son coming home from a losing effort, acting quiet and depressed. What if he blurts out, "The coach is so stupid. We could have won the game but he hardly played me at all. He played some spastic who can't even dribble the ball. How can he possibly not see how good I am?" What should you say? Anything special? Nothing at all?

Let your son say what he wants to say. Let him get rid of his thoughts and emotions. If he is emotional, he won't be able to listen to your advice at that moment anyway. When you feel he is ready, ask questions for him to ponder, rather than telling him how to behave or think: "Why do you think you aren't playing more?" "Have you been going to every practice?" "Do you show up on time, or even ahead of time?" "Do you try as hard as the other kids?" "Do you listen when your coach is talking?" "Do you respect your coach?" "Do you suppose the coach is trying to motivate you, or get you to work harder? Maybe the coach just wants to see if you can keep your head up when it's tough." "Did you think that hanging your head and acting depressed or angry showed the coach you cared? Maybe he thought it meant you weren't serious or tough."

If your child is having a conflict with a coach and is frustrated, lend a receptive ear and ask questions that will help the child discover a solution. You cannot take care of the problem; he or she must solve it. The young athlete must try to understand and change the coach's perception of him or her.

The necessity of getting an authority figure to believe and trust in him or her is a major value of the sport experience for your child. Belief and trust must be earned; they are not readily given away. When your child is frustrated at an inability to attain them, you must remind him or her that coaches generally love their athletes and will do what is best for them and the team. But your child must realize he or she is not the team, just one part of the team.

Finding a Good Coach

The best coaches for many sports are found in the schools, where the programs are well funded and your child has every opportunity to develop. In these sports there is no choice over who coaches your child. Your child must adjust and get along with the assigned coach.

Some sports, however, are still primarily dominated by coaches and teaching professionals not located in schools. These sports include golf, tennis, swimming, gymnastics, and skiing, depending upon the community. In these sports, parents must find a quality coach for their child.

Where can you find a good coach? Is there a coach or teacher who will do what is best for your child? Is there a coach who really knows how to get your child excited about sport? Is there a coach who shares your values?

It is well worth your time and energy to find out if there is an outstanding teacher-coach available for your child. Find out if the coach knows how to develop young athletes. A coach who has been successful with advanced athletes may not be best for your young child. Find out if the coach likes teaching young athletes. Is he or she someone who can really get excited and enthusiastic? Is he or she a coach who will add to your child's interest in the chosen sport?

You don't want a coach initially who is mainly interested in getting your child into competition, or one who only emphasizes winning. You want a coach who will help your child develop a great attitude toward playing. Your child should be excited about going to lessons or practice and should still be excited when coming home. If your child wants to show off new skills to every guest who enters the house, you know he or she is having fun and the coach is effective.

A good coach will help children feel good about themselves and their sport. Whether your child becomes a star, an average athlete, or gives sport up for another activity, you will have instilled a positive attitude toward learning.

The preceding points are some of the most important qualities to look for when choosing a coach. But do not go down the list asking the local coach if he or she possesses these qualities. Instead, ask the coach to tell you his or her philosophy and values. Then see if they agree with yours. If the coach seems "right" for your child, give him or her a chance. Observe some of the initial lessons and see if his or her actions agree with stated philosophies. Observe your child's attitude after working with this coach. Is it getting better or worse?

Davis Love (1982), one of the outstanding golf professionals in the country, has children who have become happy and successful golfers. He suggests that you find a good teacher-coach the same way you find a good doctor or dentist or lawyer.

> You ask other people—your friends at work or in the neighborhood. You don't go to the closest, the cheapest or the most expensive. You seek out golfers who have been teachers and got good results. Ideally, you want a pro who teaches a lot. You don't necessarily want somebody who's a good shop merchandiser or who's the best player in the area. You want somebody who's a specialist in teaching—a pro who spends all day, every day on the lesson tee. That's a pretty good sign right there he's a good teacher. After all, if you're looking for an accountant, you don't want somebody who also does photography and plumbing on the side. Ask around and find someone with a reputation for teaching—period. (p. 20)

Summary

The interactions between parents, coaches, and children present a challenging triangle. They can be filled with invigorating and beneficial opportunities for growth or stifled by jealous conflicts. The most important element is to maintain open lines of communication and to deal with disagreements privately.

Avoid emotional reactions. They seldom accomplish anything positive and may in fact ruin the opportunity for your child to benefit from the coach. Instead, keep communications open. Ask questions and understand the decision making process.

Encouraging open communications will also help your child express his or her own feelings. Create a positive environment for your child—encourage effort, initiate conversations, avoid labeling, develop the child's social skills, and provide unconditional love. Try also to find a coach who is not only skilled, but who works well with your child and helps build your child's confidence.

Parents and Coaches: In Many Ways the Same

Chapter 7

Parents and coaches are often faced with similar situations and decisions. Like effective coaches, effective parents seem to know instinctively how to do what is best for their children. Others seem to flounder as if lost and confused.

All parents who have children involved in sport will face sensitive issues, and like coaches, must be capable of dealing with them in a manner that will best balance both the long-term and the short-term needs of the child. Parents who deal with sensitive issues effectively focus on the long-term interests rather than the immediate gains of their child. Parents who do not understand this important point may let their child do whatever he or she wants right now. In return, they may get immediate love and a momentarily happy child, but eventually such decisions work to the disadvantage of both the parents and the child.

Dealing With Sensitive Issues

Good coaches learn to keep in mind not only what it takes for a child to win a game or be a strong competitor, but how it will affect that child's character and interactions with others. They know there may be a fine line between the confidence needed to play well and the swaggering overconfidence that drives others away. Such sensitive issues are even more important to parents, who play an important role in influencing their child's development.

If you wish to successfully help your child deal with sensitive issues that arise in sport, you must strive to do the following:

- Fully understand your child. This requires you to pay attention to what your child is saying and the way your child looks and feels and compare it to what your child usually says and how he or she typically looks and feels. The more you pay attention to the telltale body signals sent by your child, the easier it will be to know how he or she is feeling and learn what to do and say to get the young athlete back to a normal state.
- Understand the elements that are necessary for success and happiness in sport. Reading and understanding the information presented in this book will help. But talking with coaches, athletes, parents of athletes, and reading other books about sport also will be useful.
- Gather information about the sensitive issues discussed in this chapter to enhance the likelihood of your child's success in sport.

Most sensitive issues that will be important to your child will not have clearcut answers, so you must be able to deal with them. Effective parents learn when it is appropriate to respond one way in a particular situation and differently in another. You must be able to decide which response is best for your child at any particular moment.

The ability to make tough decisions is essential. To understand this point more clearly, let's look at some of the typical sensitive issues that parents of young athletes face. Making these decisions is never easy, but we've made some suggestions to help you decide on an appropriate strategy for resolving some of these issues.

Encouraging Humility and Confidence

Parents must help develop confidence in their children because without it, children will not survive the demands of youth sport.

For most parents this means expending a great amount of time and energy encouraging their children and teaching them to believe in themselves. You must teach your children to think that they are very good and perhaps better than most other competitors, a task that often takes months or even years. If you have ever watched a child perform poorly in competition because of a lack of self-confidence, you are aware of this need. But if you have worked with your child, you may suddenly discover that he or she is finally beginning to listen. Your child may start to believe in himself or herself, especially as he or she begins to experience success. Soon your child becomes cocky and confident, better than everyone. At this point you may have an entirely new problem. Your child may have become too self-confident, both on and off the athletic field, and now may be unbearable at home!

Chris Collinsworth, a rookie sensation at wide receiver for the Cincinnati Bengals, talked about his experience in an interview for *Sports Illustrated* (Underwood, 1981):

> When I was in the third grade, I outran everybody in the class and won a medal. When I came home, I told Mom what a fast dude I was. She said, "Don't brag." I said, "But it's true." She said, "O.K., come with me," and she took me outside the house and had Dad pace off a 50-yard strip . . . she was gonna race me. I was laughing. "C'mon, Mom, get serious." She beat me three straight. I swear. You don't mess around with Mom. (pp. 35-36)

You should teach your child the importance of self-confidence when he or she competes, but also teach the young athlete to remain down to earth, humble, and sociable in other situations.

Of course, in general the conflict does not remain as consistent or simple as presented here. Because of the competitive nature of sport, young athletes often fluctuate in confidence from day to day based upon their most recent performance. This means you must be able to respond to your child each day depending upon his or her needs. As your child comes home from a game or practice, look for body signals that could guide your response. If your child is quiet, shoulders slumped over, complaining, talking about quitting, or lacking appetite, he or she may be discouraged and lacking in confidence. You need to respond with encouragement, to remind your child of the process goals identified previously, to talk about his or her strengths, to emphasize trying hard and the need for enthusiasm. Other times, merely listen and remind your child that tomorrow will be a new and different day. But remind your child that no matter how poorly he or she performs or how little confidence the coach may seem to have in him or her, your child must believe in himself or herself.

When your child is experiencing regular success, it is possible that the child's confidence will grow to the point that he or she becomes obnoxious and overbearing at home and with friends. It may be appropriate to put your child down a bit when this happens. Remind your child of obvious weaknesses and of other athletes who are much better because they try harder. You also should talk to your child about overconfident athletes whose behavior he or she used to complain about when sport was not going so well. Remind your child how it felt to be unsuccessful. Also remind your child that friends will always be needed and they will not be there to listen if he or she treats them rudely when things are going well.

Young athletes need to realize that sport success is valued and important, but it is not bigger than life itself. They must learn that they are not more important than others just because they are successful in sport. You must help your child find balance between no confidence and too much confidence. To do this, you must be alert to your child's state of mind and respond to his or her present attitudes. If your child is too cocky, help him or her to become more humble. If your child is not confident, help build his or her confidence by accurate praise of strengths. Encourage your child to be realistic in assessing his or her strengths and weaknesses. This will help your child to maintain or move in the direction of balance and to avoid extremes of confidence, which also will make him or her happier.

Modesty is one of the prime characteristics of positive adult personalities. It is not always apparent in world-class athletes during competition, but it is a primary feature of most happy and successful athletes off the field. Athletes who feel comfortable with themselves, who do not always gain stature by calling attention to themselves or by putting others down, are respected and admired.

If an athlete is good, his or her accomplishments will speak for themselves. Successful athletes do not need to brag about their skills. Good athletes gain recognition by making others feel important, thereby indirectly raising their own self-esteem. For example, such athletes talk about the great shots their opponents made, which makes their foes feel good and simultaneously establishes their own competence.

Children learn to praise others by the examples parents and other adults set—the compliments paid to others, jokes told on oneself, and mistakes that are openly admitted. Children and adults who are achievement oriented but who can admit mistakes will be able to feel good about themselves and simultaneously make others feel important.

Encouraging Independence and Assertiveness

Success in the world of sport, and for that matter life in general, often depends upon an individual's ability to display a healthy level of assertiveness. Assertive behavior consists of standing up for one's rights without violating the rights of others. Assertive people feel comfortable expressing thoughts and beliefs honestly and openly while showing respect for others. Nonassertive people often violate their own rights because they fail to express their thoughts and feelings, and others take advantage of them as a result. In competitive sport, such people can be devastated.

Some young athletes hold irrational beliefs that lead them to act nonassertively in play:

- I might get injured if I play assertively.
- I might hurt other players if I play assertively.
- I'm not confident enough to play assertively.
- "Nice people" are not assertive.
- Assertive players are dirty players.
- Assertive players are "hot dogs."

All children should be raised to feel comfortable about expressing their feelings and expecting others to treat them with respect, listen to them, and take them seriously. They should never have to feel guilty about expressing their feelings, desires, and opinions. These are basic human rights. Of course, in the process of teaching your child to stand up for these rights, you must be sure to teach the child that others have these very same rights. Your child must understand that his or her freedom must not infringe upon another person's rights to those very same freedoms.

The goal of assertive behavior is to communicate honestly and directly. Assertive individuals make choices for themselves without harming or being harmed by others. Clinical work with athletes has shown that often the frustrated, self-defeating, overly sensitive athletes are those who will not allow themselves to be assertive. Fortunately, assertiveness is learned and can be developed in the early years of life. Teaching children to be assertive can help them to learn to take responsibility for their own lives and in the process raise their self-esteem. Children can learn to be assertive if assertive behavior is rewarded when it is appropriate. They must be encouraged to be independent and self-reliant. Parents should avoid praising children for being passive and submissive. Children should be encouraged to deal with stress, rather than to avoid conflict. When conflicts occur, especially between siblings or playmates, children should be taught the importance of standing up for their own rights.

To promote assertiveness in your child, you can do the following:

- Emphasize each day the desirability of healthy assertive play.
- Look for occasions on which your child attempts to play assertively and then reward such attempts.
- Constantly provide verbal encouragement for intense, enthusiastic, hustling efforts.
- Encourage your child to speak up and express personal opinions.
- Praise independent and self-reliant actions.
- Avoid praising passive and submissive behaviors.

This is not to suggest that children must carry assertiveness to the point of being obnoxious to be successful in sport. Sensitivity for the rights of others must not be overlooked or eliminated. Being obnoxious during competition may help a child win in a sport contest, but lose in life. Obnoxious children usually do not have many friends, for they are not perceived as caring much about others. They may be ostracized by both children and adults. If they do make it to the top, they may have some friends, but those friends will remain only for as long as the athletes are successful.

We do not believe that parents should be encouraged to raise children to be obnoxious. But we do believe children should be raised to be assertive, for it is important to happiness and success. Assertiveness, however, does not eliminate sensitivity for the feelings of others. There are situations in which individuals need to be assertive and *place themselves first*, and there are times to be sensitive and place the needs of *others first*. All athletes should be brought up to be capable of deciding when to display these behaviors.

Both boys and girls need to learn assertiveness. To be successful in sport, children must learn to stick up for their own rights. Consider the example of Andrea Jaeger, a top woman tennis player (Wheeler, 1980). Around the age of 12, a neighborhood kid stole Andrea's bicycle. She ran home to her father, a little bit scared, and in tears told him about the theft. She pleaded with him to get it back for her. Instead, her father told her, "No, no, Andrea. You have to stick up for your own rights. You go get your bike back." And she did!

Teaching your daughter to be assertive can be particularly difficult. In order to be successful in sport, she must be assertive and skillful. But there is no doubt that during adolescence, a girl's assertive behavior can bother some peers. When she plays hard and without fear, speaks up for her own rights, or goes "all out" when competing, it can result in temporary problems with other girls and boys. Have faith. Eventually the result will be admiration, success, and a child who has learned to be responsibly assertive.

You must teach your child that certain assertive behaviors considered acceptable in sport will not be tolerated and may even be punished when done off the playing field. Your child must be taught the specific situations in which assertive behavior is and is not appropriate. Your child must also be taught that the purpose of assertive behavior is to attain some specific goal—to win a contest within the limits of the rules. *Your child must never be taught to intentionally harm others*, even if it can lead to success in important contests. A sport contest should never become more important than the mental and physical health of the participants.

Controlling Aggressiveness

Most players and parents accept the importance of healthy levels of aggressiveness to success in sport. Experts generally agree that aggression, at least to a limited extent, is natural in human behavior. At birth, the aggressive drive is present and has an instinctive value in self-preservation. But as we mature, aggressive behavior is shaped to a great extent by the environment.

Parents play the dominant role in teaching responsible aggressiveness by providing rewards or punishments for aggressive behavior. Without always intending to do so, some parents indiscriminately reward or punish their children for all forms of aggressive behavior. If only appropriate aggressive behavior is rewarded, then it will be the form of aggression used most frequently.

Children also learn to be aggressive from reinforcement received during their interactions with friends and other family members. For instance, a child may hit a playmate (intentionally or accidentally) and the playmate may then give up a toy. The hitting was rewarded because the child gained the desired toy. When faced with a similar situation, the child is likely to hit again. The more frequently this aggressive behavior produces the desired results without negative consequences, the more often the child will be aggressive.

Children may also imitate the aggressive behaviors of others such as friends, relatives, and attractive and dominant individuals they see on television, including athletes. If children view aggressive behavior and can justify its occurrence, they will probably imitate it. You must help your child recognize when aggressive behavior is appropriate and when it is not. Otherwise, he or she may imitate all forms of aggression.

When children observe their parents being aggressive, they often copy them. Research has determined that aggressive parents set an aggressive model for their children and as a result have aggressive offspring. Interestingly, permissive parents also tend to have more aggressive children. This seems to occur because even though permissive parents neither reward aggressive behavior nor act as aggressive models, children know that they will be allowed to get away with aggressive behavior and that it will produce results. Children may interpret the fact that their parents witnessed and did not punish their aggressive behavior as a sign that aggressiveness is appropriate.

Finally, parents should allow and reward aggressiveness only when it is within the rules, socially acceptable, and not dangerous to others. Many young athletes will need special help learning to understand the differences in acceptable and unacceptable behaviors on and off the athletic field, particularly athletes involved in contact sports.

Helping With Shyness

Shyness is a mental attitude that predisposes people to be extremely concerned about the social evaluation of them by others. As such, it creates a keen sensitivity to cues of being rejected. There is a readiness to avoid people and situations that hold any potential for criticism of the shy person's appearance or conduct. It involves keeping a very low profile by holding back initiating actions that might call attention to one's self. (Zimbardo & Radl, 1981, p. 9)

Most parents want their child to be self-confident and outgoing. Few want their child to be extremely shy. But some parents inadvertently develop shyness in their child.

To avoid developing shyness in your child, it is important to understand how shyness is learned, although a tendency to be shy may be genetically determined. In some children, shyness develops as a result of negative experiences or imitation of a shy parent or sibling. Shyness can be particularly well learned if parents reinforce shy behavior when it occurs. Shy behavior is most commonly and easily rewarded unknowingly by parents when they praise a shy child for being "nice," "well behaved," "perfect," or "quietly cute." Many shy children receive far more attention of a warm and friendly kind when they remain quiet and removed than when they are verbal and considered a bother or a nuisance. Other children are shy because they have not learned the necessary social skills for effectively interacting with others. Still others learn to be shy because they are rightly or wrongly labeled as shy.

Some specialists who study shyness feel that two conditions in contemporary society foster the development of shyness. These are *isolation*, with its resulting loneliness, and increased *competition*, with its increased demands for high achievement motivation. Certainly parents play a crucial role in determining the degree to which their offspring experience either of these conditions.

Finally, some children learn to be shy in response to specific *situations* and people who are perceived as threatening because of their potential for *evaluation*. Thus, shyness is learned by

- imitating a shy parent or sibling;
- being rewarded for shy behavior;
- lacking social skills;
- being labeled as shy;
- being isolated and lonely;
- facing increased competition and demands for high achievement motivation; and
- being exposed to situations and people that threaten evaluation.

The reason parents intervene on their child's behalf is often because the child is too shy to express his or her own feelings. Dr. Philip Zimbardo, a leading expert on shyness, has stated that he has yet to meet a person, whether 4 years old or 84 years old, who sees shyness as a personal asset. Rather it is seen as an affliction, an unwelcome trait that forces people to shrink from life (Zimbardo & Radl, 1981).

Young athletes who are shy will be at a disadvantage in many ways:

- They will have trouble meeting and enjoying new teammates and coaches.

- They will find it difficult to communicate with and develop positive relationships with other athletes.
- They will be unable to perform assertively.
- They will not speak up for their personal rights when teammates, opponents, or coaches take advantage of them.
- Others will not recognize their personal strengths.
- They will become extremely dependent on others and be unable to withstand peer pressure.
- They will overcontrol their emotions.
- They may develop excessive anxiety or embarrassment.
- They will become self-conscious.
- Clear thinking and focused concentration may be difficult for them.
- Others may believe they are condescending, unfriendly, or arrogant, which often leads to greater isolation and shyness.

If you have a shy child who you would like to help become more outgoing and confident, there are several things you can do.

Create a Positive Environment.   One of the best things you can do is to expose your child to a wide variety of other children and experiences. Invite other children over to your house. Whenever possible, create situations where your child is older than the children with whom he or she is playing so your child will be in the leadership position and receive positive responses. Playing with younger or less skilled children will increase the chances of your child feeling more in control and more confident. In contrast, always playing with older or more skilled individuals may add to your child's feelings of frustration or lack of ability. As the child becomes more confident, mix the groups, so that experiences are available to be both the "star" and the learner.

Avoid Labeling Children.   Parents often create a self-fulfilling prophecy by referring to a child as shy. If intelligent people like Mom and Dad frequently label a child "the shy one," there is a good chance the child will live up to the expectation. Soon shy behavior will occur in situations that will cause other adults to label your child as shy. Eventually the problem becomes more difficult to reverse.

Develop Social Skills in Your Child.   Getting along with others and being liked are skills to be learned just like other sport skills. Children do not automatically know how to act. They must learn how to give compliments, listen attentively, show interest, smile, or ask questions. They may not even know how to show or express excitement or happiness.

You must help your child learn these social skills. Intentionally or accidentally, your child will learn from you. Research evidence tells us shy parents tend to have shy children. If you are shy, you must teach your child how to be different. Your child will probably model your behavior, so you may wish to work on overcoming your own shyness.

You may also find it useful to ask yourself about your own background if you are shy. What did your parents or friends do that helped shape you into a shy person? Did they constantly put you down when you tried to voice an opinion or ask a question? Did they reward you for putting yourself down or for not saying anything at all? Were you encouraged to be quiet because your parents didn't have time or were too tired to listen to your thoughts? After reflecting on your experiences, you may wish to treat your child differently. Encourage him or her to feel confident and accepted.

Help Your Child Initiate Conversation. Help your child to realize shyness often results from a feeling that others would not be interested in what he or she has to say—a feeling that is usually wrong.

The hardest part of most conversations is taking the risk of starting the discussion. Many children are hesitant to say anything, even something as simple as "Can I play?" "Could you use another player?" or "I'd love to shag some balls."

Role playing can be an effective way to help children learn to join in. Imagine a variety of specific situations. Let your child practice being outgoing. Remember, being assertive is okay.

Encourage Your Child to Try. Encourage your child to believe it is better to speak up than to be left out and lonely. Tell the child that it is worth the risk to ask to play even if he or she is turned down once in a while. A shy child will often feel being safe and avoiding criticism are better than speaking up and risking rejection. In doing so, the child also loses the chance of being praised or recognized.

Give Unconditional Love to Your Child. A child who is shy will typically have low self-esteem. Parents have a very significant impact upon the development of self-confidence and esteem. One simple way you can help is to make sure your child realizes that criticisms and reprimands are a result of your love and are directed at understanding and changing behaviors. They do not mean your child is bad or not loved. Your love must be unconditional.

There is little doubt that many children will suffer from shyness if parents don't put a special effort into preventing it. Parents should understand the specific mistakes that can lead to shyness and use the strategies presented for reducing shyness. Shyness will be a definite liability for your child, particularly in a competitive endeavor such as sport. Unless parents are willing to take a role in preventing or eliminating shyness, they run the risk of leaving their children prisoners of their own shyness.

Providing Guidance Versus Allowing Independent Performance

A child must be able to think for himself or herself to achieve success in sport. Your child will need to be able to self-direct both mind and body in highly competitive situations.

Most parents are well aware of this need to let their young athlete "fly freely." But parents also have justifiable reason to be concerned over too much independence too soon. A totally independent child traveling around the state or country can indeed get into serious trouble in today's society.

You must strive to help your child learn to direct his or her own life. However, you must also encourage responsible decision making in your child so he or she will continue to seek out and listen to your guidance.

Quality coaches also face this conflict. They must develop their athletes so they remain coachable, seek advice, and listen to instructions. At the same time, their athletes must be independent and self-disciplined enough to fend for themselves by becoming self-motivated learners and self-confident individuals.

Parents, like coaches, must spend time and energy attempting to help their developing athletes comprehend the fragile balance of these two needs. Young athletes must appreciate that going too far in either direction could be detrimental to their future development in sport.

Parents must control their emotional desire to be needed, listened to, and respected to ensure that their child can grow and prosper. A child must be allowed to take personal responsibility and exert independence to encourage achievement and to develop self-respect. You should also remind the young athlete that he or she can depend on you to provide valuable insight and direction. You must encourage your child to seek a balance between total independence and total dependence to achieve in sport and in life.

Communicating With Your Child About Competition

Parents, like coaches, can have a great effect on children's performance simply by what they say. The right words at the right time can give children the extra push they need to excel; the wrong ones can discourage and hold them back. Therefore, it is important to consider how to best talk to your child about competition, whether he or she wins or loses.

Communicating Before Competition

Children, like adults, need positive communication before they compete. Their attention should be focused on the process of competition and skill itself, not on the outcome or the opponent. Positive attitudes about their upcoming experiences will make their endeavors much more satisfying.

Children who have been practicing and exerting great effort to acquire skills should be reminded that their practice will pay off. This is their chance to try to do their best, to challenge themselves and not worry about anyone else. Their attention should be on enjoying the competition and on their performance improvement. The goal should be to learn something, no matter what the score. They should be totally absorbed in the event itself.

A parent who believes a child needs a pep talk before competition is often mistaken. It is usually much later in your child's sport experience that he or she may need a pep talk to get "psyched up" for competition. Most children who perform below their ability level during competition do so because they are already overly excited. Children and adults enter into competitive sport with a certain amount of excitement and anxiety. This increased arousal can have a positive effect on performance if it makes an athlete more alert and ready to perform. The old phrase "he was really 'up' for the match" may refer to this increased excitement and physiological or psychological readiness for competition. But be careful not to make the mistake of psyching your child "up and out" of good competitive readiness, because too much of a good thing can destroy performance. Too much arousal can cause an athlete to focus too narrowly or lose concentration, reducing performance. "Psyching up" is one thing, but it often results in being "psyched out."

If your young athlete is about to compete, and you believe your child is too psyched up and too anxious, you may be able to help him or her. There are several useful techniques that you can employ and that he or she can learn as well:

- Offer support and encouragement.
- Remind your child that he or she is well prepared.
- Believe in your child and act confidently.
- Encourage your child to focus on what he or she wants to do rather than worrying about what might happen.
- Discuss past good performances.
- Stress the competitive experience or process, not the outcome.
- Remind your child of his or her personal goals.
- Encourage positive visual imagery.
- Encourage positive thoughts and self-talk.

Communicating After Competition

Children sometimes are not able to communicate their feelings to adults. As a result, important experiences often remain hidden. This can be especially true when you were not able to attend a particular competition and you want to discuss it with your child. How do you respond when your child walks in the door? What can you say to break the ice? How do you find out how the day went? You certainly don't want to say "Did you win?"

You may want to start the conversation by asking, "How did you do?" This question leaves it open for your child to say "I really concentrated on my overheads, and hit them all. But I didn't quite win." Or to say "I played great, and won." Or anything in between. You have left the full range of responses open.

Sometimes you don't even need to ask. Your child's body language and behavior may do a great deal of communicating if you are alert to them. For example, your child may come home after a game and walk in the door very quietly, saying "hi" so faintly that he or she can barely be heard. The child may go to his or her room, or take an extra long shower. Chances are your child's sounds, postures, and attitudes when he or she walked in the front door were packed full of information. Your child was trying to let you know it wasn't a very good day. He or she may continue to walk quietly, body slumped over, and not say much during dinner. Your child may not want to talk right away. Give the child a chance, but if he or she is reluctant to talk, wait until he or she is ready.

Keep your eyes open and your ears alert. It doesn't take a genius to solve your child's problems. More than anything, your child needs a loving parent who will understand and encourage, and who will provide an experienced perspective.

Your child may need a sense of closure after competing, especially after a loss. After a particularly discouraging loss, your child simply needs you to be near. The child doesn't need or want to talk immediately. This may be difficult if it means a long and silent ride home in the car. After a short time, when your child is ready, he or she will talk. Simply listen and provide support until the emotion and disappointment subside. Provide a little humor or a hug until he or she is ready to start talking about the performance and thinking about the next game. Later, talk with your child about the events of the practice or contest. Be sure you talk *with* your child, not *at* him or her. A parent who talks at his or her child simply tells the child how he or she feels about the child's performance, how the child should feel about it, and what the child had better do about it if the child ever hopes to succeed. This dogmatic approach keeps the parent's confidence intact, but never allows the child to think on his or her own. On the other hand, a parent who talks with his or her child asks how the child feels about the performance, listens to the child's response, and then either accepts the child's response totally or presents personal insights and discusses them with the child. He or she then encourages the child to make decisions for future action. This type of communication encourages the child to personally evaluate the experience and learn how to analyze his or her performance.

There are many ways not to greet your child after competition. For example, at a recent junior tennis tournament, a young father was observed talking with his 12-year-old daughter, Mary. She had just finished second playing in the tournament for 14-year-olds. She was elated. She had finished much better than anyone expected and had competed against girls several years older. Many players were gathered around congratulating the finalists when suddenly Mary's father, hoping to seize on a "teachable moment," turned to her and said, "Your backhand really did you in!" Mary was crushed. She had come in second, was disappointed, but felt good to have made it that far. Now suddenly she was embarrassed—had she "blown it"?

It would have been better for her father to have said nothing. This was not the time for teaching, and especially not for critical comments in front of her friends. Later his ideas might have been welcome!

Another example was provided after a middle school basketball game. The child's team had won the game but the child hadn't played in the contest. The child left the locker room feeling excited and happy about the win, proud and looking forward to his greeting from his mom and dad.

When he reached his parents, though, the child's smile quickly turned to a frown. His dad said: "How can you be happy when you didn't even get in the game? With your attitude you will never become an athlete. You ought to be upset. The coach is so stupid it's ridiculous. I can't believe you didn't play. You're better than anyone on the team."

The father would have been better off to greet his child with cheerful enthusiasm, shake the child's hand and talk about the great game and the great plays. Suggesting a victory celebration would also have been an effective idea.

Questioning strategies are useful for postperformance discussions. For example, the following questions might help you focus on the positive aspects of the experience:

What was one good thing you did today?

What did your opponent do well?

How positively did you think while you were performing today?

What did you learn today?

What should you work on so you can perform better next time?

What did you really enjoy today?

It is especially important to keep your emotions out of the discussion, because this is not the time to try to teach your child. Listen, be supportive, and ask questions that might foster growth and development. Take a positive approach. Often your child will ignore what he or she has done well and will dwell on the errors. Emphasize to your child that he or she does some things well and has the ability to improve, and that with continued effort and concentration, he or she will become even better. A positive outlook toward the future is critical.

For effective communication after competition, follow these guidelines:

Don't

- make a child feel ashamed or embarrassed.
- talk without listening.
- criticize the child's or team's play.
- attack the child's coach or teammates.
- try to correct the child's mistakes.
- say anything discouraging.
- respond emotionally.
- say "I don't want to hear any excuses."
- look or act as if you are embarrassed by your child's performance.
- focus only on winning or losing.

Do

- "read" nonverbal clues of how your child is feeling.
- listen attentively to your child when he or she is discouraged— don't say anything until the child gets all his or her emotions, feelings, and thoughts out.
- display love and understanding.
- let the child know you are proud of him or her for trying and giving his or her best.
- ask questions that might focus your child's attention on positive aspects of the game.
- encourage hope for the future.

Summary

Parents and coaches share many of the same joys and frustrations. As children experience the elation of success and the self-inquiry of failure, they need adult guidance. You must understand your child, as well as the elements that produce success in sport.

Encouraging humility and confidence is essential to developing happy children in sport. Acknowledge your child's success and reinforce the effort that it took to be successful. This strategy will also help to develop independence and assertive behaviors. The goal of this assertive behavior is to communicate honestly and directly. If your child has difficulty being assertive, help him or her become more confident and less shy.

Honest and open communication is essential as a child learns to make decisions and to accept the responsibility for those decisions. Talk with your child about his or her experiences in competition. Help your child to deal well with both success and failure.

Coaching Your Child

Chapter 8

Many parents believe that they make the best coaches for their child. This may be true, but on the other hand, it may not be a good idea for either you or your child.

You think like an adult—your child thinks like a child. You love your child—your child loves you. You have authority—your child has little or no authority. These factors mean the possibilities for communication problems and emotional difficulties are ever present when you try to teach your child.

What are the most important problems you can anticipate when setting out to coach your own child? What are the most likely conflicts? What can you do to avoid or resolve these conflicts? Your ability to prepare for these situations will be crucial to your success with your child. In the section "Deciding if You Should Coach Your Child" we'll mention possible problem areas. But first, you must consider sport from your child's point of view.

Perceiving Sport
Through Your Child's Eyes

Children who are not yet teenagers tend to view the world around them from an all-or-none perspective: "I'm a super athlete" or "I stink at sports." "I'm a good hitter" or "I'm a crummy fielder." Because of this, you need to get your child feeling good about himself or herself from the outset. You would be far better off to build a young athlete up with a little white lie than to be so realistic you destroy enthusiasm. Be careful not to overemphasize results or the importance of winning or losing.

Positive feedback is crucial to your child in these developmental years. Be sensitive and patient with your child until he or she is in love with practicing and playing. Only gradually should you start to introduce corrections and structured practices, because constant corrections can discourage almost any child.

Perceptions of children, especially teenagers, may be quite different from yours. If your child is just getting started in sport, peer perceptions can be critical. It may be important to him or her to dress according to peer standards, to act in a certain way, and to project an acceptable image. It may or may not be acceptable or "cool" to play with a parent. Be aware of these perceptions and plan your strategy carefully.

Some children who are just learning a new sport will not want to be embarrassed. You may want to find a time and place for practice where you won't be observed by your child's friends. A good way to see if your child is bothered by opinions of others is to observe the child after he or she makes a bad mistake. Where does your child's head turn? Does he or she look around to see who is looking? Does he or she then get upset? Does your child want to practice only his or her best skills? If so, these are signs that the child is concerned about the opinions of others. There is an old saying that for some children "it may not matter what they think they are, or even what other people really think they are. What matters is what they think others think they are." Be sure you lead them to believe they are special.

Some children will not develop an interest in sport until they reach their teenage years. It is not uncommon for a 15-year-old to think it is too late in life to learn a new sport. You must help your child realize it is never too late if he or she enjoys it and is willing to be patient and persistent. Try to get your child to find a friend to practice with, someone who has similar abilities and interests.

Perhaps even you would be a good partner, especially if you are just learning the sport. You can learn it together, from the beginning. You can set the perfect model for your child and prove it isn't too late to learn. You can demonstrate that enthusiasm and patience pay off. But beware—you won't be able to fool your child. You must do what you say!

Deciding if You Should Coach Your Child

Think carefully as you make the difficult decision of whether or not to coach your child. You must be willing to accept your child as he or she is regardless of initial ability or motivational level. This attitude will allow you to understand your child and help him or her move forward.

As a parent-coach, if you allow your dream to dominate, trouble will usually follow. You will push too hard and too early. Your child may get turned off or may play for you, rather than for himself or herself. The result is almost always a child who dislikes sport and who is unhappy in the future.

Sport may greatly improve the quality of your relationship with your child; it may also destroy it. You must ask yourself honestly if you can communicate with your child. If not, are you willing to start over when you start coaching your child? This is a must if the experience is to be positive.

One thing that all effective coaches learn is that they have to communicate with young athletes at their level. Parent-coaches who do not succeed at this task will fail in their undertaking and probably disrupt their family life as well.

Does Your Child Come First?

Does your child really want to play sports? Do you want to coach your child because you feel you can best help your young athlete accomplish his or her desires? Or are there other reasons?

Many parents coach their child because they dream of their child becoming a star athlete. Have you dreamed of being the star coach of the star player? Or the famous parent of the star player? The dream isn't necessarily bad, especially if your child shares the wish for stardom. But you must decide upon your priorities. Will having you as a coach help your child realize his or her dream? Coaching your child will demand a commitment from both of you. Be sure you are willing to make it. As long as you are coaching, other things such as your chosen career, family trips, or free time may need to be given a lower priority.

Can You Teach Well?

If you want to coach your own child, reflect on the past for a moment. What were the teachers like from whom you enjoyed learning? Try to remember. How did teachers you disliked treat you? Take the best from the past and add it to your own style—and avoid the worst.

Be honest with yourself. Do your child a favor and think about teachers who turned you on. If you can't remember, watch a few practice sessions of a youth sport team in your area. Observe a physical education class at your child's school. See what turns children on and what bores them. What you learn will help you and your child.

Will you teach in a way that will be interesting to you, or to the child? It is much easier to do what interests you. You must, however, get into your child's world. Be enthusiastic rather than serious. Speak in a vocabulary your child understands. There is no need to impress. Your job is to communicate and teach.

Does your child like to talk with you about playing and how to play? When he or she does, be careful you don't talk too much. Most young athletes would rather play than talk or listen. When your child is ready to talk about strategy and technique, he or she will let you know. When your young athlete asks, be ready to respond. Your response to a specific question should show that you know what you are talking about. A child learns a lot about sport early in life today. If you are unsure of what you are talking about, don't try to fool the child.

Can You Keep Emotional Control?

Coaching your child will be an emotional experience. Sport is emotional. Can you handle the emotions? Ask yourself honestly. When you stop playing, can you sit down to dinner and forget about frustrations or failures that occurred on the playing field? If your child plays poorly, will you blame him or her later at home? Will you steal the glory of success and embarrass or blame your child over failure?

Can you keep your child's success or failure in perspective? Be sure you know the answers to these questions before you start coaching your child.

Your child will learn how to cope with various stresses in life from you, in great part through imitation of what he or she hears you say. It is critical, therefore, that the child hear you say the right things! When you are in a stressful situation and your child is watching, speak out loud so your child can learn how you cope with the situation. For example, if you play in a tennis tournament and lose while your child is present, shake hands with your opponent and congratulate him or her, then remain calm and happy. Talk to your child about how much fun it was to compete, about the great shots you hit, and about how you can't wait for your next chance to play. Also be sure to talk about the skills you will practice in the meantime to prepare for your next tournament. Finally, stop talking about tennis and move to another topic to demonstrate putting competition in perspective. This role modeling is best done enthusiastically, with no hint of lecturing to or teaching your child. Make it as indirect a learning experience as possible. Children often learn best when they are unaware of learning.

If your child sees you effectively dealing with stress and anxiety, he or she will be able to imitate your methods. If, on the other hand, you lose control, the child may imitate you by also losing control, and as a result develop inappropriate coping skills.

Coping skills can be learned just like any other skills. If you help your child practice anticipating how he or she will respond in different situations, you will be providing an opportunity for the child to learn to cope effectively. To return to the tennis example, you can sit with your child the night before you play in a tournament match and talk about situations that might occur during play and how you would handle them. You might imagine losing the first three games and staying composed; losing the first set and then coming back from behind; or double-faulting four times in a row and coming back to concentrate and serve well in the next service game. In this way you can demonstrate how to anticipate situations in which you momentarily lose composure and then regroup to play effectively. You also can emphasize the advantage of being prepared for every possibility and the good feeling of being on top of any situation.

You will probably never find an endeavor that tries your emotions the way sport does. The more involved you become with your child's career, the more this point holds true. Your child will experience many highs and lows in sport, and you will share in both the elation and the suffering. The key is to maintain perspective through the joy and the pain.

When your child is doing great, you will burst with pride. When he or she fails, you will hurt. You will want things to be better. You may become blind to what fairness really is. Every official's call against your child may seem wrong. You may view athletes who defeat your child as cheaters or poor sports. If your emotions go uncontrolled, you may embarrass yourself with a public outburst that reveals your innermost feelings. You may make a fool of yourself and shame your child.

You must strive to maintain emotional control in such situations. It is far from easy. For a brief moment, nothing will matter but your desire to protect your child. But remember, emotional control is a skill that can be learned. If you do not already possess good control, try this strategy: (a) When you feel emotions rising, tell yourself to stop and wait 30 seconds, (b) take a deep breath, and (c) make some positive statement about the situation. Learning to control emotions and set good examples requires that you first be able to recognize emotional situations. Once you sense a difficult experience, use rational, calm statements to help control the moment.

When you are watching your child compete, you may have to really work to control your emotions. If you are hurting for your child, discouraged, or disappointed, try not to let your facial or body expressions show it. You never know when your child will look over at you for support. When he or she does, it is usually best to be calm and controlled or encouraging and enthusiastic, even though this may be difficult when you are hurting on the inside.

You must remember what is really best for your child. Of course it hurts when others are celebrating and your child is crying. But sport is an endeavor where you either win or lose. Your child must learn to savor the wins, live with the losses, and learn something from both. To do so, the child must be able to control his or her emotions. Parents who are unable to maintain control can expect emotionally uncontrolled children who may never learn to respond in a healthy manner to competitive pressures.

Can You Remain Enthusiastic?

For years coaches have been put on pedestals. Coaching may be a glorified position, but it is not an easy job. It demands energy, time, commitment, and knowledge. Many successful coaches allow the athletes they coach to become the focal point of their lives. That can be particularly tempting when the athlete is also your son or daughter. Most coaches see their athletes at games and practices two or three times a week. But if you coach your own child, your contact doesn't end after practices. Will you have the energy to practice with your child each day after a long day at work? Imagine hearing the following greeting every day: "Come on, Dad. I've got all the equipment. Hurry up and get changed so we can go to practice. We've got great weather. I really need to work on a few things that have been giving me trouble."

How are you going to respond? Are you willing to get excited and find the energy necessary to respond to your child's enthusiasm? Or will you turn your child off? Will you think of yourself and say "No way, not today. I'm tired, and you don't need the practice anyway."

If you are not able or willing to do what is best for maintaining and developing your child's interest and enthusiasm, you may need to get someone else to coach. Be honest for the good of your child—and for the health of your relationship.

Are You a Good Enough Athlete?

Do you have to be a talented athlete to coach effectively? What if you are only average or even below average in physical skill? Is playing ability or teaching ability more important?

Not all great coaches were great athletes. Being a successful athlete is not a prerequisite for you to be an effective coach. You must, however, understand your child's sport or be willing to work diligently to learn about it. You must be able to observe your child's performance and perceive when and when not to make corrections. Most importantly, you must make corrections in such a way that your child will love learning and improving. All the knowledge in the world is useless to a coach who fails to make it meaningful to the athlete.

If you are still not convinced you can help your child, consider this: Many talented athletes fail miserably as coaches. Their skills may have come easily to them so they don't understand how to correct the problems of others or how long it takes to learn a skill. They may lack patience. They may only enjoy working with highly talented children. Many fail to encourage athletes or to praise them for consistent effort, and give rewards only for winning results. For your child, positive results may be a long way off, and effort should be the primary reason for encouragement. It can be an advantage to have been a talented, experienced athlete, but only if you can appreciate the problems and struggles of a child who is not so talented. Such parent-coaches are hard to find.

Once you decide to coach your child, be honest with yourself and with your child. Admit if you are not a great player. Let your child know you are going to try to be a great coach by learning all you can about the sport. Even if you are not skilled, you can demonstrate by practicing correct form while standing still. It would be better to perform specific skills at game speed, but even slow motion is helpful. Other options include studying the performances of athletes on television or on video tape or observing talented athletes who live in your community.

Being a great athlete is not generally important when you coach your child. What is important, however, is that you not embarrass your child by pretending to be a talented performer rather than learning to be a great coach. Therefore, you must periodically reevaluate the importance of your skill level to your child, especially in team sports where peer pressures and expectations can be so strong.

Finally, you can learn how to play better yourself while teaching your child. Learn and practice along with your child. Take a segment of every practice session and allow your child to teach or evaluate you. It will help you remember what it is like to be a learner, and it may help your child understand what it is like to teach.

Are You Willing to Continually Seek New Information?

If you think you can coach your child, you probably already have a healthy dose of self-confidence, but there is a fine line between having self-confidence and thinking you know it all. If you think you do, forget it. You can coach for 50 years and not know it all.

Your child won't be the only one who will make mistakes. You will too. You must be willing to view mistakes as an enjoyable part of the experience. You had better be able to believe in yourself while honestly admitting mistakes you have made and be willing to search for a better way when one is not readily available.

As your child's coach, you must keep up with new developments. You must be willing to read books, go to clinics, and talk with other knowledgeable coaches and teachers about training, practice organization, and competitive strategies.

Following is an example of what often happens to coaches who are not willing to seek answers to problems:

Child: *I've been shooting the way you taught me for 3 months now. I'm not getting any better. I don't think we're doing it right, Dad!*

Dad: *Don't you dare question me. Try harder. Just keep doing it and believe in me. If you would spend more time doing instead of questioning, you would probably be better by now.*

This response usually occurs when the parent-coach cannot explain the child's lack of progress. Rather than admit a possible error or problem with the prescribed technique, the parent-coach uses power and control to stifle the child. Stagnation and frustration instead of growth and happiness will be the result. You must be willing to search for information about your child's sport and share it with him or her to achieve credibility as a coach.

There are a number of other questions that you will have to answer to help you determine whether you should even try to coach your own child. These may be the most important questions, because you must consider your child's feelings and the feelings of other children in the family.

Does Your Child Want You to Coach?

Like it or not, sometimes a child will not want to be coached by a parent. Don't take it personally. Many children take up sport for the friendships that go with the involvement. Your child may want to learn with friends and may feel that having a parent as a coach will interfere with those friendships. If your child has such feelings and you can afford a different coach, it may be best to honor your child's request that you not coach him or her.

Sometimes it is easy to find out if your child wants you as a coach. He or she may simply ask, "Would you work with me every afternoon? I'd like to learn how to play better and you could help me." If your child does not ask, but appears interested in learning, you might take the initiative by saying "Would you like to have me teach you how to improve?" If your child says yes, and you don't know everything about the particular sport, admit it, and explain that you will have to learn together.

Can You Be Objective and Avoid Making Comparisons?

Many parents try to motivate their children by comparing them to brothers, sisters, relatives, or other athletes. Is this an effective approach? Does it do more harm than good?

This approach may work for some children. Often, however, the positive effects may be short term, with the negative effects lasting much longer. In addition, the wrong type of motivation may be instilled and children may resent both parents and those they are compared to for the rest of their lives.

The Brett family, which raised two major league baseball players, provides a poignant example. Jack and Ethel Brett, the parents of four boys, provided early experiences in sport for all of their sons. Two of them, George and Ken (Kemer), became highly successful in professional baseball. However, their initial interactions with their parents exemplify the strife and frustration of many families. In an interview (Garrity, 1981) George reported:

> I hated my Dad . . . He'd say, "*Bobby* wouldn't do this," or "*Kemer* wouldn't do that." I was intimidated. I was scared to death of him. (p. 55)

> I called him up once from New York . . . My brother was with the Pirates then, playing a doubleheader in San Diego. I think Kemer won the first game and got a hit. Then he pinch-hit and tripled off the wall in the second game. So my dad said, "Get any hits today?" I said, "No." He says, "George, your brother's a *pitcher* and he's outhitting you." And he started screaming at me on the phone. . . . I just hung up the phone. Then I threw the phone against the wall, tore it out of the wall. I went and slugged the full-length mirror. Shattered it! Threw a chair against the wall. . . . He made *constant* comparisons. I wasn't as good as my brothers. I *never* would be as good as my brothers. (p. 63)

George didn't know this at the time, but his father actually was telling the rest of the sons that George was the best player of all of them. Fortunately, the Brett brothers remain friends to this day.

Parents must decide if sport requires isolating brothers, sisters, and parents. A lifetime of resentment and constant comparison may be the result. Far too often, athletic families break family ties because of these pressures. Parents must decide if athletic achievement is worth this price or if these efforts can be moderated. If you can't manage these issues, maybe you shouldn't think about coaching your child.

Do You Know How Siblings Will Feel?

In families with more than one child, a parent may have to look carefully at the problems associated with coaching one of the children, as we mentioned previously. Be honest with yourself. Are you more excited about the child who shows an early interest in sports than the rest of the children? How are your other children likely to feel if you spend all your time coaching one child? Will you provide the same enthusiasm for some other activity they are excited about? Will you share in their triumphs and failures? Are you adding fuel to a sibling rivalry?

Parents who have more than one child are well aware that rivalries do exist. These parents often ask: Are such rivalries healthy? Will they separate children for life? Will a sibling rivalry encourage a love or hate for competition? What advice is available when one child is more successful than the other? Is envy a problem?

Parents sometimes complain because their young children do not always get along. In general, the closer the children are in age, the greater the rivalry, with the most intense rivalry occurring when children are about a year apart. Sibling rivalry is normal and is often healthy. When children disagree or fight they are learning important negotiation skills that can help them resolve conflicts later in life. But sometimes rivalry can go too far. Problems can develop when the emotional fights are not balanced by periods of affection. Parents should be concerned when rivalries include frequent and excessive tantrums, jealousies, hostility, criticism, or physical aggression by one or both children.

Sibling rivalry often stems from a child's fear, often unjustified, that parents love another child more. Frequent rivalries are most severe when they occur between the two oldest children, who often display the greatest difference in character and temperament.

The oldest child, often intense and highly critical, may try too hard to be the perfect number one. He or she may occasionally get discouraged and withdraw. Don't put too much pressure on the oldest child; such a child usually puts enough pressure on himself or herself. Be supportive and make sport a fun experience. The second-born child is often more easygoing. He or she may try to beat the older child, and often succeeds. The sibling rivalry is heightened when such competition exists.

Parents must anticipate this situation, because coping with it can be difficult. Help each child identify his or her strengths and weaknesses, so that siblings learn to appreciate each other. When rivalry leads to a fight, stay out of the squabble as long as the children are old enough to fend for themselves. If not, parents should help the children in their search for identities. Sit down and talk with each child about why the sibling is causing a problem and explore a better way of responding. When you do get involved, don't try to arbitrate the fight while in the middle of it. Parents can also lose sight of good common sense when they're upset emotionally. Calm down first.

Keep sibling rivalry in perspective. It can be a problem, but it is not the end of the world. Such feelings are natural, and if kept in balance may spur a child on to great accomplishments.

A classic example of a positive resolution to a sibling rivalry involved Amy Caulkins' younger sister, Tracy, the world record holder in several swimming events. Amy, a successful swimmer herself, recalls,

"I really couldn't stand the pressure. I really couldn't stand to be in the same room with her."

Amy recalls the 1977-78 swimming season when her little sister set World and American records, one after the other. "Any little thing got to me. I thought she was getting anything she wanted. Even from our parents."

Since that time, Amy's attitude toward her sister has changed. She has learned to value both her own skills and those of her sister. Today she says she would just as soon watch Tracy swim as swim herself. It was a long, and sometimes rocky road for Amy to get to that point. However, "My parents understood and tried to be helpful, but I guess what it really took was just maturing."

Amy still talks about the first time she was recognized. "My parents were sitting in a restaurant in Berlin and two guys from the Greek water polo team came up to them. 'Are you Amy's parents?' they asked. That was the first time my parents had ever been asked that. Usually it was 'Are you Tracy's parents?' "

There is still pride in Amy's voice when she tells the story. Somehow one gets the feeling it was then that Amy realized she was as much a Caulkins daughter as her talented sister.

What would Amy Caulkins say to an older brother or sister who has to live with a younger sibling always outdoing them?

"I'd just have to tell them to hang in there and do their best. Nobody can expect more from you than your best. That's where I had trouble. Everyone was expecting more from me. You have to learn to be your own person.

"Maybe I just thought about it too much. I should have been proud of Tracy and I am, now. I guess it just comes from growing up."

Amy Caulkins grew up and learned. But it was a difficult lesson to learn. As she now says: "Things are so much better when you are cheering for your sister." (Power, 1980, p. 6)

Despite the difficulties, sibling rivalries should not be considered negative. Most parents who have more than one child in their family involved in sport strongly agree that the advantages of growing up in a family with another motivated athlete far outweigh the disadvantages. They have each other to talk with and share joys, sorrows, and thoughts on competition. Such supportive friendship is hard to find elsewhere. The impact may be even more beneficial when they play the same sport and have each other as partners for practice, conditioning, and travel. A controlled sibling rivalry can be a source of inspiration, understanding, and motivation hard to find outside the family.

Should You Coach Your Own Child if You Are a Coach?

Some parents really are coaches. If you are the high school coach, local Little League coach, or maybe the local golf or tennis professional, what should you do when your child is ready to start playing? Should you be the coach? Can you handle it? Can your child deal with it? What problems can you expect?

You cannot easily make an objective decision about coaching your own child. You love your child and want to do what is best. You think you are a great coach. You believe in your way of coaching. You really can't think of anyone who would be better for your child or for the other children. But coaching your child is not like coaching someone else's child. When practice ends, you will not go your separate ways. You will go home together. If your child is skilled and plays regularly, others will criticize you for giving him or her special treatment. Fail to play your child when he or she is part of a team sport, and your child will perceive it as unfair punishment. Either way, someone will suffer.

An All-American athlete recently talked to us about a coach he had earlier in his career. For him, the coach was the best he ever had. Yet the coach apparently failed miserably when he tried to handle his own child. This All-American runner said:

> When I was 9 or 10 I had a coach who was great. We all respected him and learned a lot from him. He had a son my age who also ran. I don't know many people more enthused about sport than this coach. His son was a skilled athlete who was one of the best at his own sport. The coach was great with other children, but with his own child he pushed and forced it too much. He didn't let him grow and enjoy the sport and mature with it as he grew older. He tried to force the discipline and dedication too soon and lost the fun of the game. Now his son totally avoids all sport involvement.

A similar situation exists for the local tennis or golf professional. Club members will expect the pro's child to be skilled and to love playing. When this doesn't happen, it must be the pro who is to blame: "You can't be a very good professional teacher if you can't even teach your own child." Clearly this situation can cause a coach to feel added pressure.

When you feel pressure, you may become a different coach. You may not be the effective teacher you usually are. To coach your child successfully, you must keep your emotions under control. If you can't, another coach may be in order.

Of course, the moment you make this decision some people will criticize you. They will argue that you do not have enough confidence to coach your own child. Stand your ground. At least you have enough confidence in yourself to make a tough decision that will provide a positive sport experience for your child.

Coaching your own child is a difficult situation, at best. There are many problems, but there are also many joys. It will force you and your child into a special closeness. You will always have something to talk about and share. There will be emotional ups and downs. You will be criticized and praised. Once you decide to coach your child, you must talk openly with him or her about what it will be like. Talk about the potential jealousies from teammates. Tell your child you might at times be tougher on him or her than others just because he or she is your child and you want what is best for him or her. Tell your child you think you can handle it. Then ask your child how he or she feels. Ask if he or she can handle the pressure of having you as a coach. Does your child wish to play for you? If he or she does, make it clear that if the child ever changes his or her mind you will understand, you won't take it personally. And make sure you don't!

Following in Famous Parents' Footsteps

Having a father or mother who is a star in a sport does not necessarily mean the daughter or son will follow. Joe DiMaggio's son never played organized baseball and Mickey Mantle's son had only a brief fling in an instructional league. Stan Musial's son was athletically gifted, but chose to run track at Notre Dame instead of playing baseball. On the other hand, several baseball children have followed in their parents' footsteps: Dale Berra, son of Yogi; Bump Wills, son of Maury; Buddy Bell, son of Gus; Bob Boone, son of Ray; and Steve Trout, son of Dizzy.

Most of these parents had little time to spend with their children because of extensive sport travel. When asked, they helped. Often they advised mainly on the mental aspects of the game. In general, they tried to provide advice and encouragement. Most admit now that they love watching their offspring excel in sport.

Famous mothers seem to have a similar experience with their daughters. They are well aware of the perils of trying to follow the career of a famous parent. The situation must be handled gently. But if the child loves the sport and wants to play, the experience can be rewarding and successful. Two highly successful athletes, Maureen Connolly Brinker and Peggy Kirk Bell, have daughters who excelled in their sports, tennis and golf, at the University of Virginia and the University of North Carolina.

Some highly successful professional athletes encouraged their offspring to play their sport but emphasized different values than the ones they espoused during their playing careers. Dave Schultz, one of the most often-penalized players in the history of the National Hockey League, offered the following advice for his two sons:

> If my two boys embarked on a hockey career, I'd tell them to do the opposite of what their father did. Get out of hockey or tell the coach or owner they are not going to earn their living by beating heads. I don't want them to go along blindly with

management the way I did. I also would tell them that they will have to make big sacrifices if they want to get to the top, but that there is more to success than the almighty dollar. (Schultz, 1981, p. 15)

Children of former stars have many questions and concerns. Some ask, "Will my dad or mom love me if I want to be an engineer instead of a tennis player?" "Will I ever be as good as Mom was?" "I don't want to think of him as a pro, he's just my dad." You must convince your child that your love is unconditional, that you loved playing a certain sport, but that you will love the child no matter what he or she chooses.

Some children try to emulate their famous parents, others back off. It's the parent-child relationship that is the key. Children should be proud of their parents. They can be happy following them into sport if they have a chance to express their own abilities and needs.

Some parents are particularly supportive and open with their children. Jack Nicklaus, perhaps the most famous name in pro golf, is an excellent example. His son, Jack Jr., never felt his father's accomplishments haunted him, which is particularly noteworthy since a "Junior" has the added potential of identity doubts because he carries the same name as his famous father. Jack Nicklaus's support is perhaps best seen in the way he followed his son's football career. He missed only one of Jack Jr.'s games at Benjamin High in 4 years. That record included a Friday night in the middle of the World Series of Golf in Ohio when Jack Sr. piloted his private jet to North Palm Beach, Florida, for a Friday night game and returned to Akron to tee off on Saturday. The mutual understanding and support of the two Jack Nicklauses are reflected in the fact that Jack Jr. decided to concentrate on golf in college.

Daughters of famous fathers and mothers also feel the pressure. However, for most daughters of famous fathers, the importance of being a successful athlete is tempered because society does not seem to place as much emphasis on sport success for girls. Jean Musial, daughter of baseball's "Stan the Man" Musial, a Hall of Fame member, even claims she did not realize the magnitude of her father's career until their family was a part of the television program "This Is Your Life" when she was 12. She did, however, acquire a field hockey nickname at the University of Richmond—"Jean the Girl"!

Parents who have been successful in sport have a special situation to manage. Their children are often expected to be great, and the result is a kind of no-win situation. When their children dislike sport, the parents get blamed for pushing them. On the other hand, if the children love sport and attain success, many accuse them of playing only for their parents.

Fortunately, many parent athletes have handled the situation remarkably well. Their thoughts and strategies can be useful for any parent, especially those who are former athletes.

Frank Tripucka, a star quarterback at Notre Dame University, went on to play in both the National and American Football Leagues in the 1950s and 60s. He and his wife Randy raised six boys and a girl. The twins, Heather and Tracy, came first, followed by five boys. The children's sport experiences are noteworthy. Tracy has been an assistant basketball coach at the University of Utah. He previously set many scoring records at Lafayette University. Mark played quarterback at the University of Massachusetts. Michael Todd stands third on the Lafayette all-time scoring list. Timothy played basketball for Fordham University. Kelly played basketball for Notre Dame and now plays for the Detroit Pistons of the National Basketball Association. Christopher is a high school kicking star in New Jersey. Heather once scored 56 points in an intramural basketball game. A story for *Sports Illustrated* (Newman, 1981) described Frank Tripucka's approach to raising his children.

> Frank Tripucka put up a backboard in the yard and installed lights so play could continue until 11 p.m. most evenings. "My thing was, don't sit around the house doing nothing and end up getting yourself in trouble," Frank says. "I never pushed them, but I wanted them to get involved in something. Some fathers will teach their kids to bat a ball or to shoot baskets, but I never did that. I just gave them the equipment and let them play." (p. 34)

Nancy Lopez, a Ladies' Professional Golf Association great, argues that it may be an advantage to have a father who is a golf professional, but it can work the other way too because many pros push their children into the game. She discussed in a magazine article her experiences playing on the University of Tulsa golf team with two other women who were daughters of club pros.

> I saw what pressures their dads exerted on them, and I think it hurt their progress. The girls wanted to play professionally, but they have not enjoyed as much success as they might have. I have to believe it was because of the parental pressures they faced in their early years. (Lopez, 1981, p. 136)

Nancy talked about a brief period during her high school years when she felt her mom exerting too much pressure on her. When she came home after a bad round she felt her mother's unhappiness. Fortunately, her mother quickly realized what was occurring, and changed their interaction.

Nancy's dad was also very supportive, and he was able to encourage her talent without using pressure:

> There is a fine line between support and pressure, and my dad walked the line better than anyone I know. He started me playing at 8 and always tried to make the game enjoyable for me. He wanted me to practice, but never forced me into it. He had little ways of making my practice fun, such as holding a bucket for me to hit wedge shots at, and saying "try not to make me move when I catch the ball." I'll never forget my first pair of golf shoes. I loved to hear the sound those spikes made walking across concrete. It made me feel like a golfer. (Lopez, 1981, p. 136)

Nancy also suggests that parents can help their children by providing lessons, etiquette, and proper equipment. It doesn't take much to encourage a child when parents give their support and enthusiasm.

Parents should not get discouraged if their child does not show constant improvement. Some children have skills that develop early, like Nancy Lopez, and then level off for what seems to be a long period of time. Her dad never discouraged her. He simply reminded her that if she wanted to improve, she would have to keep practicing. He provided that needed support and encouragement, not pressure!

Deciding When Your Child Has Outgrown Your Coaching Ability

You've worked with your child for several years. You've done a great job. Your child has really progressed. Should you continue coaching your child? When is the time to step aside? There are no magic answers to these questions. It is a difficult decision, but there are some cues you can use to help you.

First, if you feel constantly frustrated because you have no idea how to continue to help your child improve his or her skills, it may be time to look for outside help. You may decide to let someone else take over the coaching completely. You may decide to spend a week with your child visiting a highly successful coach. The visit may be free or it may be expensive, but it will probably be worth it. Have the coach give a detailed evaluation of your child's skills. Solicit suggestions for improvement. Ask the coach to speak openly with you and your young athlete about what it will take to continue to advance. Listen attentively to what is said, and don't argue or disagree just because what you hear is different from what you have been doing. Take some time to think about what the coach says and analyze the suggestions for a day or two. Present your viewpoints to the coach, listen to his or her responses, and then decide on a course of action.

There is another cue that can tell you if your child has gotten too good for you. The cue is basic: Has your child stopped listening to you? When you make a suggestion, does an ugly face or raised eyebrow result? Something is seriously wrong when the child displays this type of behavior frequently. It may be you. It may be your child. Maybe it is both of you! If learning and practicing are no longer enjoyable, the situation must change quickly or it is time for another coach.

What if you and your child both decide it is best for him or her to play for someone else? Help your child find a coach who shares your values and beliefs. Careful decision making at this point will prevent many problems later. Select a coach your child can be happy with and support them both. Avoid criticizing the coach if your child becomes unhappy about a particular situation; the same thing could happen if you were the coach. Most importantly, give the coach a chance. If you are hurt that your child is not playing for you, try not to show it. You must consider your child's needs before your own.

Summary

Teaching and coaching your own child can be a very difficult or very rewarding experience. In either case, the parent-child relationship is likely to be tested.

In order to make a good decision about the possible effects of your own coaching, you must be willing to answer some tough questions. Will I be good for my child? Can I be fair and objective? Could someone else provide better guidance?

You must also consider the impact of the coach-athlete/parent-child relationship on your family life. Will there be serious sibling rivalries? Will open communications prevail? Will I be able to motivate, discipline, and reward my child fairly? If you can honestly answer each of these questions, you will probably have a chance at being a good coach. If not, perhaps someone else should work with your child.

Systematic Practice Techniques

Chapter 9

The age at which a child begins a serious practice program depends on individual readiness and interest. Some children will be ready at a very early age, but others may not be capable or interested until they are much older. Although many professional athletes believe that it is important to help children practice, they agree it is even more important not to make them practice. For example, Tom Watson, a leading professional golfer, suggests that children should not be forced into practice until they are ready to dedicate themselves 100 percent. Once that happens, some expectation of regular practice should be established. Practice may mean working hard, but it can also mean having fun and gaining satisfaction.

Parents who help their children develop a sound groundwork of basic skills have provided the base for advanced performance if and when the child desires it. For example, Marcia Frederick, a young gold-medal-winning gymnast, did not even think of gymnastics until she was 10 years old. At 10, she happened to go by the YMCA where her father was playing basketball and saw a group of children "jumping around and stuff." She became intrigued by the activity and when the YMCA coach opened a gymnastics class, she enrolled. She loved it, and began to dedicate more and more time to gymnastics. In October of 1978, she won a gold medal for her parallel bar routine at the World Gymnastics Championship in Strasbourg, France.

There are other examples of children who decided to be serious about sport at very early ages. Tracy Austin received her first tennis lesson at the age of two. She was on the cover of World Tennis 2 years later and by the time she was 16, she had won 25 national junior titles. Her tennis began at a leisurely pace, but as with most promising athletes, the pace soon accelerated.

Each child is different. Some will make an early commitment, but others take longer to become serious about sport. The important thing to remember is that it is your child's choice, with your role being one of nurturing and providing opportunities and encouragement.

Effective Practice Sessions

When children are enthusiastically interested in an activity, they will seek opportunities to practice. And when they practice seriously, they will enjoy it. The key is to provide a systematic, enjoyable approach to skill development. In the early years or when they begin a new skill, it may be most important to allow them merely to experiment. Eventually, though, they must determine specific goals for each session and keep those plans in mind throughout practice.

Set Goals for Practice

As described earlier, the establishment of attainable goals will provide excellent motivation for your child, provide a number of potential success experiences, and also help to focus the practice. For example, if you are helping your child develop a good forehand drive in tennis, you may wish to establish a practice technique in which you hit 30 balls to the child's forehand, each to be returned within 5 feet of the baseline on your side of the court. You do not necessarily have to play a normal game, but perhaps you can make the specific drill into a game. The goal can become the challenge. If your child can now hit 10 of 30 balls within the target, tomorrow set a new goal of hitting 15 of 30 balls to that target.

The establishment of specific goals for practice not only helps focus attention on the skills to be mastered, but also provides a way to acknowledge progress. Helping your child set goals, reach them, and then reset them at a higher level is an excellent way to develop both decision making and dedication.

Make Practice Fun

Learning must be fun as well as beneficial to development. Practice sessions that are well organized and set to meet specific goals will be filled with intense effort, hard work, and good times.

Designing practices that appear to be games is fun, even though you have a specific goal in mind. For example, if you challenge a young female basketball player to a game of "around the world," you can be working on her shooting abilities from a variety of locations while simultaneously helping her deal with the problems of concentration and pressure. By setting 10 "spots" around the basket, you can help her expand her shot selection while she's having fun. When she becomes good at any one location, move it back or change her orientation to the basket. She will enjoy the challenge while developing her skills.

Another good technique for helping your child to be enthusiastic during practice is to ensure that each practice starts and ends on a positive note. If your child looks forward to playing with you because you always have a fun activity planned or a successful challenge established, he or she will treasure practice time. These fun activities can be warm-ups or conditioning exercises, but seldom involve the rigid formation typical of calisthenics. Some fun activities may even hide their real purpose. The stunts of partner wheelbarrows, crab walks, and kangaroo hops, for example, can be fun ways to develop strength and coordination, especially for younger athletes. But remember, fun and variety are important motivators.

Practices should also end on a high note. If you have been working hard with your child on a new swing with a sand wedge, practice seriously, but when it is going well, quit! The same is true whether your child is working on free throws, spikes, round-off flip-flops, or batting technique. Ending a practice with successful, fun experiences allows your child to feel good about practice and to remember and mentally rehearse those good performances.

A well-known college coach once commented that setting a specific length for practice time can ruin most athletes. Instead, he advocated setting a specific goal and estimating the time required to master it, but letting the accomplishment of the goal actually determine the end of practice.

A child who loves practice and hates to leave when it ends will return with much greater enthusiasm. Parents who run their child into the ground or end practices with dreaded wind-sprints or arguments teach the young athlete to dislike practice. A better approach would be to set a goal of always ending on a positive experience. A good rule of thumb is to *make your child quit practicing before he or she makes you stop!*

Children love to master new skills as long as they are having fun or feeling good about themselves. Some parents have found that disguised practice is the best; others believe children can understand the goals of practice and still enjoy it.

Provide Positive, Effective Feedback

Helping children learn good sport skills requires a fine balance between keeping them motivated and giving them enough specific information at the right time to produce rapid learning. Several guidelines may be helpful in structuring your feedback to children. Provide feedback that is:

- constructive, not destructive;
- positive, not negative;
- specific, not general; and
- sooner, not later.

Constructive feedback recognizes the positive aspects of your child's performance and builds on those. It should be focused on things you can see for yourself so you know your child will be able to understand what you see, and build on the present skill level. For example, you may want to tell your young tennis player: "Your forehand looks great. You get the racket back early and are really prepared for the shot. On the backhand side, you need to do the same thing. Get the racket back as soon as you realize the ball is coming on the backhand side." What a difference from someone who merely comments, "You sure have a lousy, lazy backhand!"

Keeping feedback *positive* accomplishes two things: It strengthens (reinforces) something that can be built upon, and it affirms the individual. Positive feedback tells your child how to improve or correct a problem, not merely that the problem exists. Similarly, the more *specific* the feedback, the more easily the child can change. One effective way to provide information to a young basketball player who has trouble controlling the dribble would be to say: "You're quite good at getting your hands on the ball. When you do, try keeping the ball lower by bending at the waist and knees. Use just your fingertips and you will find it easier to control the dribble." Notice how this suggestion employs a positive beginning, a specific cue, and a positive ending.

This technique is particularly effective in a practice setting. If your child attempts a skill and fails, or does not have the skill needed for a specific situation, use that time as a "teachable moment." After seeing the need for a new or modified skill, the child will be much more receptive to your comments. Thus the *sooner* you provide the feedback, the better. There is nothing more frustrating for a child than to have someone say, "Remember last week (or yesterday) when you had your pass blocked by No. 11? If you had faded back, faked right, and then rolled left . . ." It is not likely that your comments will be very meaningful at that point.

The best feedback focuses on what to do rather than what not to do and what is wanted rather than what is not wanted.

Praise Before Criticizing

If you can make your child feel good about himself or herself, that child will be receptive to your suggestions. Let's assume you really want to help your child with his or her tennis serve. As you observe the serve, you notice two major problems in execution: the ball toss and a "hitch" in the swing. There are two ways you might approach these problems. You could say, "Your serve is really ruined by that terrible ball toss. You throw the ball way out to the right and have a bad hitch in your backswing. How do you ever expect to take advantage of that topspin motion with such bad execution?" Or you could reverse this comment and make a much more positive suggestion: "Your arm swing has a beautiful pattern for a natural topspin. I bet that if you would throw the ball more directly over your head, you would feel an even smoother action and get better results."

Notice that the length and content of the comments are almost the same. But most children would rather hear the second version. If you follow the old adage of "say something good first," children will be much more receptive to your suggestions. This technique gives you a chance both to affirm their ability and encourage their effort.

The process of identifying something good first will also allow you to focus on one aspect that should be retained while also giving a specific hint on how to improve. Remember, you cannot correct everything at once. Use this progressive approach to build sound skill development.

Teach in Organized, Progressive Steps

When teaching sport skills to children, you must take one step at a time. Most skills require a good base of support. One good technique in helping youngsters is to look at their leg and hip action first. Check to see if the correct foot is forward and if the legs and hips are moving sequentially. Then build from there. Don't fall into the trap of worrying about the arms and hands first, when in fact their action is usually the result of what the trunk does first.

There are many excellent books that describe the specific techniques necessary for various types of sports. Take the time to read these books and learn about the skills your child will need to be successful. Usually at the beginning stages it is easy to guide the child's progress through sequential steps. Be sure to analyze the skills needed for success, and then build a program that will allow the development of these skills. When in doubt, check with a teaching professional to be sure that you understand the skills and can organize them into a good progression for your child.

Keep Things Active, Not Passive

Children learn by doing. It is essential that their innate desire to move is satisfied during practice sessions. Remember that the only way our bodies master skills is by repetition.

The old adage that practice makes perfect has two important corollaries: repetition is important, and what is repeated is remembered. The second point is very important because it suggests that practices must be of high quality so that the *correct* movements are repeated. For example, the young golfer must be encouraged to hit many golf balls during each session, and to hit each one as correctly as possible. It is a balance between "how many" and "how perfectly" the athlete practices.

Spread Practices Out

Most teachers and coaches know the best way to practice is to establish a series of experiences to develop skills. If your child is scheduled to practice for 5 hours per week, it may be best to spread them over a 5-day period rather than to allow fatigue or boredom to develop by spending too much time at once. This technique will promote effective learning because it gives the child time between practices to digest what has been learned, to rest, and to return with renewed enthusiasm.

Spreading out practice sessions will not only facilitate skill development but may also help prevent "burning out" a young athlete. Organizing participation by seasons and helping to develop other interests during appropriate times of the year may also be helpful. For example, many young basketball players consciously participate in other school sports such as tennis or baseball during the off-season. These additional activities not only help to develop other interests, they also help to keep the athlete in shape and make basketball more enjoyable. Of course, you must consider whether your child's interest in basketball is so intense and the competition so stiff that it might be important to play basketball year-round to keep his or her skills up to par.

Communicate by Explaining Why

Communicating with your child is not always easy. You must work at it. Your child may ask, "Why should I practice or do my homework?" Some parents simply take the easy way out and use parental power: "Because you have to!" or "Because I said so!"

It takes a little more time and energy, but it would be much better to relate the activity to attaining a goal. You might respond with "It's important to do your homework so you can get some rest and stay eligible. Remember, 'no pass, no play.' Besides, everyone looks up to you, and you should set a good example for them." For the more highly talented young athlete, you may be able to emphasize the importance of grades in order to go to college. Then listen and observe. If there is a verbal response or a facial response, or some subtle body language movements that question your reply, take the time to provide additional support. Avoid getting emotionally upset. Once that happens, little if any learning will occur.

Ask Questions

Many parent-coaches get excited about helping their child. As a result, they act as if they know everything. They think they can read their child's mind and body. Have you ever heard a parent say, "You aren't even trying. You don't care. You aren't listening. You aren't concentrating. Listen to me!'"? Instead of telling your child what he or she is thinking or feeling, ask a question. It is the only way to find out what is going on. A young athlete will usually be honest with you. When you ask, "Why aren't you doing what I just told you?" your child may tell you, "I don't understand" or "I'm confused. I can't think of two things at once. I still don't have the last thing down yet." Listen to your child's response and back up a step if necessary. You must slow down or speed up to meet your child's level of interest and skill. Don't expect your child always to adjust to you.

As your child grows, you may have to become more realistic with him or her. If your child wants to attain certain goals in baseball and yet at the age of 14 wants to go swimming instead of practicing hitting and fielding, there is a problem. Your child must either stick with the commitment or admit he or she may have to lower personal goals. There is no magic answer as to when you must be this realistic with your young athlete. But sooner or later you must be honest and straightforward.

When your children near adolescence, they may start to hide their true feelings and thoughts. It becomes even more imperative that you become a good listener during these years. If you have consistently given your children the opportunity to express feelings without fear or reprisal, you may have averted many of the potential problems.

Remember, to have effective practice sessions:

- Set goals for practice.
- Make practice fun.
- Provide positive, constructive feedback.
- Praise before criticizing.
- Teach in organized, progressive steps.
- Keep things active, not passive.
- Spread out practices.
- Communicate by explaining why.
- Ask questions.

Special Techniques for Practice

Children learn motor skills in specific ways and at distinct rates. A young athlete may have a great overarm throw but only a fair ability to catch or hit, or a child may learn to bat a baseball much earlier than "batting" a tennis ball with a racket.

There are some skills that seem to be similar across many different sports. For example, the basic skills of striking a ball overhand are similar for the tennis serve, the volleyball serve, the badminton clear, the tennis overhead, and the volleyball spike, although the way they are executed may vary dramatically. This implies that once the overhand pattern is learned, it will be easier to transfer it to a related skill than it would be to learn a completely new skill. This means that children should try many activities when they are young to provide a foundation for learning new skills later in life.

The fact that early skills may be important in later choices of sport is important as you help plan your child's practices. Some parents believe children should be encouraged to participate in several different sports. This has the obvious advantage of introducing more skills and adding variety. Unfortunately, it has the disadvantage of spreading out a child's time among different activities.

Demonstrate

Most motor skills can be effectively communicated through both explanations and demonstrations. For younger children, demonstrations should come before lengthy explanations. Children are good mimics and can learn a great deal through "monkey see, monkey do" techniques. For example, a recent practice for our softball team was filled with comments such as "Watch this . . . (demonstration)," "Notice where my hands are placed . . . (demonstration)," and "See how my fingers point down toward the ground . . . (demonstration)."

A long discourse about a skill as the first step will probably lead to boredom or confusion, but a good demonstration can set the scene and be very helpful. For example, in wrestling a lengthy discussion could be used to explain the fireman's carry takedown. However, a good, vivid demonstration, emphasizing that the wrestler should begin with a wide stance, can impart most of the important information. Through this demonstration, wrestlers can learn the principle of keeping a stable base of support by taking a wide stance. They can also be more actively involved in the learning process.

A good rule of thumb when introducing new skills is to give a demonstration to indicate the general nature of the skill, describe the skill and its techniques or applications, and then give it a specific name.

Develop a Sport Vocabulary

Each sport has its own special vocabulary. The names of equipment, players, and techniques are all important. Names for offensive and defensive systems and their components all express important ideas and concepts about the sport. In addition, being able to "talk the language" of a specific sport helps set the scene for developing skills and understanding in that sport.

Young athletes need to understand the game, the rules, and the equipment. A recent scene at a Little League meeting may illustrate this point. At the first day of Little League practice, the players had been throwing and catching for about 25 minutes when it was time for batting practice. The coach asked who wanted to be the catcher and wear the catcher's equipment. One youngster asked, "What's that thing?" The coach answered, "it's for your protection." "Okay, I'll be the catcher," the child said. As he grabbed the gear and protective cup he asked, "But what do I use to protect the other knee?"

Another example from Little League also illustrates the importance of knowing the terminology of the sport. One little boy came to Little League the first time at the first game. Since the league has a rule that everyone must play, the coach suggested that even though the boy didn't know the rules, all he had to do was make contact with the ball and run to first base. If he got to first base, he was told, someone would tell him what to do from there. The boy hit a marvelous line drive and ran to first base, then second, then third, and then suddenly ran out of the ball park. The coach caught up with him in the parking lot and asked what happened. The young ballplayer responded, "I did just what you told me. I'm on my way home. I ran to the first one, and was told to go to second. I got there and they said go to third. I got there and they said to go home! What did I do wrong?"

Understanding the rules and equipment of the game is obviously important as a foundation for establishing good skills. Examples or demonstration can help attach meaning to sport vocabulary. Show the action or object, describe it, and then name it with its proper sport term. A good description is essential; for example, "Watch this kick. Notice that you are running before and after you kick the ball, Run, and drive the ball. This is called a 'running drive.'" Such a sequence takes advantage of SDN: show-describe-name. Most terms have a logical link to the action or item. For example, a drop shot literally drops to the surface and does not bounce back up as high as expected. The spike drives the ball downward like a railroad spike. The "Wooden offense" is named for the UCLA coach who made it famous, John Wooden. Such common sense explanations will help attach meaning to the language of sport.

Make Practices Similar to Game Conditions

Good competitive sport skills must be practiced in gamelike situations because of the specificity of motor skills. Practicing a jump shot from 12 feet away with no one guarding you is not really practicing the same skill required in a basketball game with 10 players on the court.

The way a player performs during a competition is directly linked to how he or she practiced. If the player never practiced while hot or tired, he or she may not play well under those conditions. If in basketball a player has never practiced against a zone defense, the performance will reflect it. When a player is first learning a skill, practice should be as simple as possible. But once a skill is learned it should be repeated under a variety of conditions. For example, it is not sufficient to practice a basketball or soccer dribble at different speeds and in different directions; the dribble must also be practiced with someone guarding, when the player is fatigued, when the player's body must be between the ball and the opponent, and in a variety of other situations.

Because there are many situations in which a skill is executed in most competitions, it will help to vary practice environments. The following elements should be varied in practice if you expect them to change in different competitive situations.

- *Environment:* Vary the size of the playing area, the surface texture, noise, spectators, temperature, artificial lighting, and other elements.
- *Technique:* Vary the types of skills required to accomplish the same goal, practice with or without defense, with opponents of differing skills, and so on.
- *Strategy:* Practice different strategies, including your own as well as the opponent's offensive and defensive techniques.
- *Individual conditions:* Practice when fatigued, hot, hungry, or stressed.
- *Equipment:* Practice with different types of equipment if it is likely to be used in competition. Vary the weight or texture of the ball, playing surface, and so on.

The importance of quality practice cannot be overemphasized. All players can benefit from systematic and motivating practices. The key is to structure practices to meet a specific goal and to guarantee that striving to meet the goal is meaningful.

Use Television as a Learning Tool

Young athletes can learn from watching sporting events on television, which can present an effective demonstration of the techniques and the language of different sports. In particular, television presents the opportunity to watch the performance of the best athletes in the world. Television certainly shows the rewards given to successful athletes and also shows that children can be good athletes even at a very early age in many sports.

Parents can help their children learn by watching sporting events with them. Talk about the joys of seeing skilled performance and the pleasures of success in sport while watching. Praise your child if he or she demonstrates these skills, and praise the televised athletes who have worked hard to attain them.

If you observe good sportsmanship, comment upon it. If you notice poor behavior, be sure to discuss it as well. Do not wait until a crisis and then say, "If I ever see you do that you will never play again!" Rather, show appreciation and admiration for behaviors you value. Your child will be much more likely to follow this indirect positive advice rather than instructions on how or how not to behave. Direct commands are often difficult to follow and may result in rebellion. So deliver your message, but be subtle.

You can have an enjoyable learning experience with your child by identifying with an athlete you are watching on television. You can pretend to be one athlete while your child pretends to be a teammate or opponent. Turn off the volume and discuss the strategy. Lay out your game plan. As the contest begins, try to think aloud the thoughts of each athlete. As the contest continues, discuss how you could each alter your strategy. Follow the contest carefully. After the event, evaluate each other's strategy and discuss productive and ineffective plans. Compare your strategy decisions with those of the televised performers. Encourage your child to analyze situations and strategic decisions.

Television can become a great opportunity to interact with your child when you share a sporting event in this manner, but you must watch it actively rather than passively. If you are to benefit from television, you must concentrate and think. As a result, you will learn and so will your child.

Televised sport also provides opportunities to study the techniques of top athletes. Watch how a player concentrates on the requirements of the task at hand. If your child is a football lineman, pick out the appropriate player and watch what he does. Don't always simply observe the ball carrier. A great deal of the excitement in football occurs in the line. If you are attempting to help your child develop skills, carefully watch the slow-motion replays of the top players. For example, if you are helping your child improve in golf, watch the careful backswing of Pat Bradley or the putting of Nancy Lopez. Watch and feel the rhythm of the swing, the concentration of the performers. Notice how the top players use a specific routine and visualize their upcoming shot before they ever swing. Note the set-up, the waggle to get comfortable, and the release of undesirable tension. Observe their composure even in tense and highly competitive moments.

Observing the careful and consistent preparation of professional athletes is important. If your child can learn to visualize himself or herself in specific situations, it can also help in real physical practice situations. Have your child imagine pressure situations or real-life game experiences during the next practice session. If your child can learn to solve the problem in imagination first, the actual practice or performance will be much better.

The use of television to establish good models of behavior can be quite effective. As children grow older, they may benefit from good professional models, not only for their skills but for their competitive attitudes. Television can provide an excellent way to bring these professional models into your household.

Be sure to help your child choose a model or models that reflect your values. As we emphasized earlier, consistent experiences that reflect your values are important in selecting coaches, teammates, and even professional models. There may be some professional athletes whose behaviors you would not wish your child to imitate, so you need to spend time observing the models with your child and provide opportunities to discuss what is observed. This open discussion is perhaps the most important skill to develop with your child.

Allow Play of Video Games

The recent advent of electronic video games provides even another opportunity for new challenges in which children can develop good skills. Many of the video games are excellent for developing visual tracking skills, hand-eye coordination, and various strategies. These games can help children develop a sense of the value of practice, unlike some of the other popular games of luck.

Select video games that encourage children to plot strategy. It is not enough to merely fire rockets, jump barrels, or dodge monsters. Youngsters should be encouraged to describe how they are going to "attack" the problem. In addition, if you encourage them to be persistent and to take logical risks as they become more skilled, children will begin to develop high levels of achievement motivation.

Computer or video games can be good diversions and can teach some skills, but too much play can be harmful. If children become "addicted" to them, or choose to play them for long hours instead of practicing real sport skills, video games will probably be a negative influence. With careful use, however, video games can be challenging, stimulating, and a good way to learn some skills.

Again, some special techniques to use for practice are the following:

- Demonstrate.
- Develop a sport vocabulary.
- Make practices gamelike and specific.
- Use television as a learning tool.
- Allow play of video games that require strategy.

Summary

Systematic practice techniques are essential to good skill development. They are also important if children are to be given an opportunity to learn to enjoy both practicing and playing.

Several techniques will help adults create positive learning environments and fun practice sessions. Using specific goals, demonstrating, and making practices close to game conditions will help encourage quality effort and the development of skills. Other keys to effective practice include providing positive and effective feedback, praising before criticizing, teaching in organized and progressive steps, keeping practice active, and spreading practices out over time. It is also important to stimulate a young athlete's sporting mind by explaining why a skill is done in a certain way by asking questions, and by helping to build a sport-specific vocabulary. Use television and video games as tools to improve techniques.

If young athletes are actively involved in the learning process, they are likely to develop a positive attitude toward both play and practice. A positive attitude will create an atmosphere in which practice is fun and rewarding rather than a penalty. Remember, quality practice is the key to sport success.

Understanding and Analyzing Skills

Chapter 10

Understanding sport is important for both parents and children. Information about techniques, rules, strategy, and mental control is essential for success in sport. As Pat Bradley, the 1986 LPGA Player of the Year, states:

It takes an honest and complete understanding of yourself and your golf game to become a top contender on the professional golf tour level. Most players on the tour have a basic knowledge of technique or they wouldn't be here. Some players refuse to stop analyzing and make the game too complicated. Once a player understands technique it is necessary to leave it alone and get on with learning about yourself so that you can play within yourself and use your mind and emotions as a friend rather than an enemy.

You must start by learning to analyze and understand the sport skills your child will need, and couple that with the unique personality and emotions of your child.

Helping the Child Understand the Skill

If you wish to help your child be a good athlete, you must be able to break down skills and analyze their parts. You must be able to describe each skill, strategy, or technique to your child. In order to do this, you must be able to decide what to tell your child, and when. The first step is to decide what is the most important thing to say. Often there are many problems or suggestions apparent to you, but you must decide upon the one most important thing to mention. Too many points will only confuse the child. The second step is to decide how to describe the skill. It is not enough merely to be able to diagnose a problem or set the next target for skill development. You must be able to communicate the solution effectively and to plan practices efficiently.

The intricacies of high skill level, or Olympic-calibre performances, are tremendous. People spend lifetimes studying the mechanics and strategies of champions, but the basics of most sport skills can be summarized and understood by almost everyone who is genuinely interested. These basics should be understood by both children and adults.

Principles of Movement

Six principles of sport skills are identified in this chapter. These six principles can be used to teach all sport skills to young athletes. These principles will allow skills to be broken down so that specific parts can be practiced. Once the parts of the skill are modified, the total skill can be put back together for improved performance. The six principles are these:

1. Sufficient strength and flexibility are necessary.
2. Sequential joint action produces maximum force.
3. Movement over increased distance and time produces more force.
4. Longer levers produce more force.

5. Stability is the key to producing force.
6. Equal and opposite reactions govern direction and force of movement.

Principle 1: Sufficient Strength and Flexibility Are Necessary

The human body is designed to use both strength and flexibility to produce coordinated movements. Without adequate strength and flexibility, a young athlete cannot move effectively and efficiently. The first principle is therefore to check that adequate strength and flexibility are available for the skill. This principle also suggests that for most children increasing the specific strength and flexibility needed for a particular skill will produce improvement in the skill.

Strength is produced by applying force across joints in the correct order. Flexibility is the capacity to move the body and its parts through a total range of motion. The relationship between strength and flexibility is obviously very important. If a child is allowed to increase strength only, the result will generally be a reduction in flexibility as the muscles become tighter and stronger. However, this does not have to be the case. Flexibility exercises should be built into any training program so that the muscles maintain their elasticity and ability to stretch.

Help your child understand that strength is the result of the capacity to apply force and that increases in strength will produce changes in speed and power. In order to produce muscular contractions, most sport skills require that actions begin from a bent or flexed position. For example, a jump ball, volleyball spike, or back handspring all begin from a semicrouched position. This allows the body to explode to a straight position for maximum force at takeoff. A football punt is another good example. The kicking leg moves backward as the first forward step is taken. The leg is then quickly brought forward and straightened to produce maximum speed and force at contact with the ball.

Children who wish to be successful in athletics need to be strong. Their strength is developed by use of specific muscles in relation to the demands of the particular activity. Your child can develop strength that will be very useful to his or her sport performance. Both boys and girls show marked gains in strength as a result of training that includes both general conditioning and sport-specific activities. If the sport requires long expenditures of strength or power, training should be for muscular endurance. If the sport requires short, explosive bursts of strength, training should be of higher intensity.

The amount and intensity of strength training should, therefore, be specific to the sport, age, and ability of your child. Many adolescents need specific strength training, whereas younger athletes may require more general programs. Pam Shriver, an outstanding tennis player, has suggested that her rapid improvement as a young professional player was due to strength training. She worked specifically on arm and leg strength 4 days per week during her early years on the tour.

Many parents are concerned about the effect of strength training on their daughters. Pam Shriver's example shows the benefits of strength training. The fear of girls becoming "muscular" or unfeminine as a result of strength training is not realistic. Boys can become more muscular after puberty, when increased androgens are produced. However, females do not possess these hormones at the same level as boys. In fact, with the onset of menstruation, there are only limited quantities of androgens in a girl's body. The benefits of strength training for girls are improved skill development and a firmer body, and for most, strength training will not result in a more muscular figure.

The importance of strength to produce force and flexibility to allow production of force cannot be overestimated. The body must be flexible and able to move through a full range of motion. This ability to move freely and fully is important not only to produce force and power but also to help ensure safety. Children should learn to stretch both before and after practice to protect their bodies and to allow full force to be produced.

Principle 2: Sequential Joint Action Produces Maximum Force

Power is produced in sport by moving specific muscles in the correct sequence with the right timing. The phrase "sequential joint action" describes how forces are added together to produce the most power in sport skills.

All active body parts must contribute to the motion to produce maximum power. This combination must occur in a specific sequence or order so that the force or speed from one body part can be added to the next action. For example, many children have difficulty jumping high because their arms and legs do not work together. Children may have problems in jumping because they are pushing off with their feet only and not using the knee and hip extension for force. Similarly, many children cannot throw a ball well because they do not rotate at the hips and shoulders before the arm is allowed to come through. The classic beginning throw is an arm action only, rather than a step forward and rotation before the arm extends.

The sequence of action of the joints of the body is very important. In the overhand throw, the weight must be transferred forward, followed by hip rotation, then shoulder, then finally the arm action itself. The forces that are produced by each of these actions are added together to produce the maximum thrust. If the shoulders come through too early or if the wrist snaps too soon, the sequence will be broken and less force will be produced. In general, the sequence must begin with the part of the body in contact with the ground and move progressively to the other end of the body.

As a teacher of skills, you must be able to analyze which joints should be used and in what order. If your child wants to jump higher or throw farther, you must know which joints need to be bent (flexed) first and then extended to produce the needed force. You must also have a feeling for the rhythm of the movement and the sequential timing of each joint action.

Some young athletes seem to lack the force to produce effective results even though they seem to have the proper sequence of movements. For example, Bill swings a baseball bat pretty well, but he never seems to hit the ball hard. Sally has the same problem with her golf drives. She has a good swing, but the ball just doesn't go anywhere. Both of their problems may be that their swings are not timed properly. In striking skills, power is determined by how fast the object, for instance a bat, club, or racket, is traveling when it hits the ball. This is controlled by the last joint in the sequence, the wrist, and its influence on the club or bat. In throwing or kicking, the speed of the object will depend in great part on the speed of the hand or foot when it makes contact with the ball.

To increase speed or distance, check for the principles of sequential joint action, strength, and flexibility. These control the speed of the last joint or the object that makes contact with the ball. For Sally and Bill, you should check the speed of their swings. In addition, you may also wish to check their grips. A weak grip may cause the object to lose power at contact, whereas too firm a grip may reduce the flexibility necessary to produce maximum speed.

Principle 3: Movement Over Increased Distance and Time Produces More Force

Skills that require a great deal of force or speed demand that the movement be extended as long as possible. This extension occurs by moving through space, or by stretching out as far as possible, or by using as much time as possible to produce the movement.

The backswing in sport skills is a good example of this principle. Most people move their arm or leg back to stretch the movement out and allow more time and distance on the forward swing. The backswing in a tennis forehand or a football punt allows the arm or leg to move through a longer distance and establish a straight or firm position at the moment of contact with the ball. The backswing in most sport skills serves to get the arm as far behind the body as possible so it will travel longer and cover more distance as it builds speed before contacting the ball. Similarly, the use of the forward stepping motion in throwing allows the body and arm to travel a greater distance and have more time to develop additional speed and force.

You can check three key points when observing skills to see if the principle of distance and time is being used: (a) There should be a complete and full backswing, (b) there should be a forward step and transfer of weight, and (c) there should be a full limb extension at release or moment of contact.

The reverse of this principle of force is also an important concept in sport. In catching or controlling a ball, the athlete must control the force of the ball. An athlete who wishes to catch a ball must absorb the force. In catching an oncoming object, the more body parts that are allowed to flex and the greater the distance over which this flexion can occur, the more force that can be absorbed or controlled. When catching a ball, therefore, it is best to begin with the arms extended in front of the body and the feet in a forward-backward stride position. This allows the body to "give" with the force of the oncoming ball. Similarly, an athlete running or skating forward and wishing to stop quickly should plant one foot first and then step forward while bending the knee of the other leg. This allows the body to "give in" and absorb the force and forward motion.

Principle 4: Longer Levers Produce More Force

Objects or implements such as bats, golf clubs, and lacrosse sticks generally produce more force than the body alone. This principle is the result of the principles related to strength, distance, and time when an object is used to produce force. Objects that extend the length of the arm provide more force than the arm can produce itself because the object and the arm act as one lever and can move faster than the arm alone. A lacrosse player using a crosse can "sling" a ball much faster and farther than it could be thrown by hand.

In sports that use implements the length of the object itself will influence speed and power. In general, the longer the object the faster its end will travel, and therefore the greater the force. For example, in golf the longer clubs, woods and long irons, will travel faster at their ends and therefore produce more force and propel the ball farther. That's part of the reason players hit the ball farther with long irons than with short irons. On the other hand, longer objects are harder to control and often heavier, so be careful to match the equipment to the performer.

The larger implication of the principle of leverage is that an athlete needs to allow the body to work like a lever. Hitting a tennis serve with a bent elbow, for example, produces less force than full extension because the arm, or lever, is shorter. Checking for full extension and fast speed is an important part of analyzing a skill.

Principle 5:
Stability Is the Key to Producing Force

Effective, efficient, and skilled movements are produced by using the body correctly, and that can happen only when the base upon which it moves is solid. The human body must work against its support system to produce good skills. A tennis player on clay must act differently than one on grass or cement. The ice skater must use his or her body differently than the dancer or gymnast because of the narrow blades that serve as the base of support. Principle 5 relates to the athlete's ability to use his base of support to produce effective movement.

The base of support, the connection between the body and the surface on which it is supported, is the major interaction affecting sport. The body must be balanced yet able to move quickly. This stability depends upon three factors: (a) the size of the base of support, (b) the height of the body and its center of gravity over the base, and (c) the relationship of the base of support and the body, its posture, and the forces being applied. For example, if a gymnast wishes to balance on one leg (a small base of support), the body must be kept over the foot that is on the ground. Sometimes this requires that the arms be on the side of the body opposite the legs so that body weight can be kept balanced over the base of support.

In sports that require both balance and the ability to resist the force of other influences (e.g., blocking in football), it is important to remember each of the three factors. To maintain balance when someone is pushing against you, you may wish to take a wide stance (larger base of support), which will allow the force to be absorbed over distance, bend your knees and hips to lower the body (lower center of gravity) for more stability, and be sure to keep the head and shoulders over the feet (keep the body over the base of support).

The height of the body in relation to its base of support is an important factor in many sport skills. If you stand straight on your tiptoes, you are much less stable than if you squat down on your tiptoes. Thus a wrestler or fencer will bend the knees and hips to lower the body into a squat position and gain a more balanced position. From this position, the athlete also can produce more force. Similarly, a ski jumper must land in a flexed position, knees bent and in a squat, to absorb the force from the jump and maintain balance.

The final factor related to balance is also important. It involves the relation between the body position and its "line of gravity" to the body's base of support. The base of support is the total area between the feet or any other part of the body or equipment that touches the ground. The "line of gravity" is the vertical line through the body's center of gravity, generally located near the belly-button. This center of gravity shifts as the body's weight shifts. If you extend your arms and one leg out to the left, for example, the center of gravity moves to the left, and you must shift your hips to the right to stay in balance over your right leg.

Many sports rely on quick movements that are produced by explosive force and by taking advantage of a loss of balance. A runner may want to temporarily "lose balance" by leaning forward in the starting blocks so that his or her line of gravity is in front of the base of support (feet in the blocks). This position makes the runner fall forward to start out of the blocks effectively. For running, this lack of balance is desirable. In contrast, the handstand requires a good alignment of the body, its center of gravity, and the base of support. Learning to control the element of balance is essential in sport.

Principle 6: Equal and Opposite Reactions Govern Direction and Force of Movement

Many sport skills require the production of force by pushing something against something else. This action/reaction usually occurs when an athlete pushes against the ground or an object rebounds against something solid. A jumper pushes down against the floor to allow his or her body to "react" in an upward direction. A swimmer pushes back on the water to propel his or her body forward. A basketball rebounds off the backboard at an angle equal to the one at which it hit the backboard.

This principle of equal and opposite reactions is useful in helping young athletes understand skills. Jim, a neighbor, was trying to learn to use starting blocks in track and field. The coach had loaned him a pair but had not told him how to use them. Jim knew he should crouch down before starting. He did that. But his first action after the gun was to stand up straight and then start to run. He did not really understand that the starting blocks were there to let him push backward (rather than downward) to go forward faster. As soon as he understood that the idea was to keep leaning forward so he could extend his legs backward, his time improved greatly.

Gail, a gymnast, is another example. She could never do a headspring until someone told her she had to feel like her seat was falling over forward beyond her head before she extended her legs or pushed with her arms. Before that time, she was directing all of her force upward, instead of forward and upward.

Checking the direction of force production is one of the first steps in helping your child improve sport performance. Direction problems often result from poor body position and weight transfer as described in the track and gymnastics examples. They may also be the result of an imbalance of strengths within the body. In golf or field hockey, many right-handed players drive the ball off-target to the left because their strong right side produces too much speed and the stick or club ends up aimed to the left of the target.

Whenever a force is produced by extending against a surface, the direction of motion reflects the principle of equal and opposite reactions. To jump higher, for example, you must push *down* harder so your body will go *up* higher. Similarly, when you push your legs down and to the right, you will move up and to the left. Swimmers who move in a zig-zag path are probably pulling their arms down and across their bodies, rather than down and back. This principle emphasizes that the direction of force production controls where the athlete or object goes, a principle important in producing the most efficient force.

Summary

The six principles discussed in this chapter emphasize the key elements of skilled performance. There are many more sophisticated analyses available for each sport, but these six principles form the foundation for most skills. It is important that you understand each of these six principles:

1. Sufficient strength and flexibility are necessary.
2. Sequential joint action produces maximum force.
3. Movement over increased distance and time produces more force.
4. Longer levers produce more force.
5. Stability is the key to producing force.
6. Equal and opposite reactions govern direction and force of movement.

If athletes and coaches understand these principles, performance will be improved. As with any teaching cues, these principles must be carefully discussed and applied. When you begin to talk with your child about a particular skill, select a limited number of points to emphasize. If you try to tell a child everything you know about a skill, you will probably only confuse and overload him or her. In addition, if you as a performer or your child as an athlete try to use all of the information available at one time, you may suffer from "paralysis by analysis." Such a conscious attempt to understand too much at one time is very ineffective. Select a few key points to emphasize and identify short cue statements for each. These cues will become the building blocks of the skill. Later you can modify cues and become more specific, but for the time being, build on the solid foundation you have created based on the six principles of movement.

Preventing Injuries

Chapter 11

Much of the excitement and thrill of sport comes from striving for success and taking chances—sometimes risking injury. But there are ways to reduce the risk of injury, thereby helping to ensure happy and successful experiences in sport. The young athlete must always keep risk taking in perspective. There is no glamour in serious injury.

Proper Training

Preparation for sport is the key to prevention of injury. Your child's body is growing and changing rapidly. Each sport has specific requirements for strength, flexibility, agility, endurance, and speed, so maintaining adequate fitness is important to reduce the possibility of injury and promote correct performance of skills. A child may adopt abnormal movement patterns to compensate for a lack of fitness. The stiff-wristed baseball swing, the push tennis serve, the hop "jump shot," and many other inefficient motor skills can develop when a child is not adequately prepared or when equipment is not appropriate because it is too heavy or too big. Skills performed incorrectly are not only sometimes dangerous but often result in bad habits that mean the child must relearn the skills when he or she develops a sufficient level of fitness. This causes the young athlete to have to learn each skill twice rather than learning it properly the first time! When a child has a good basic fitness level, he or she will be able to learn the proper physical skills earlier and more efficiently as well as practice the skills more consistently.

You can help your child by encouraging him or her to train properly. A well designed training program is important for skill development and safety and should be geared to the child and the sport. There are many training programs available that will help your child attain a good overall level of fitness plus focus on specific aspects of conditioning related to his or her sport. Most sport governing bodies such as the United States Tennis Association and the National Federation of Gymnastics have special publications available for children or parents. Check with these organizations for guidelines related to conditioning and physical fitness. If there are no guidelines available for your program, check with the director of the local YMCA or high school physical education program. They should be able to give you important information for your child's fitness program.

If you are choosing a specific program, consider the following characteristics for good training programs:

- Is there an equal balance of strength and flexibility exercises?
- Are exercises paced to allow for progressive improvement?
- Does the program contain elements that seem to be linked to the particular sport? For example, if the sport requires a great deal of upper body strength, does the fitness program provide for the development of all of the necessary muscles? If the sport requires short, quick actions, does the training program emphasize this aspect?

Basic Safety Precautions

Participation in sport exposes your child to some degree of danger, either physical or psychological, but careful evaluation and planning can minimize the actual threat. In order to provide safe and positive experiences for your child, you must check the total environment. There are six key areas to evaluate:

- Appropriate equipment
- Rule modification
- Developmental levels
- Preparation for emergencies
- A safe playing environment
- Medical screening

Provide Appropriate Equipment

Carefully examine the equipment your child uses in his or her sport. It must be appropriate for his or her age, size, and skill level. More important, it must fit properly. Check to see if your child's equipment fits well and meets minimal safety standards.

As a good rule of thumb, you should generally be sure that the equipment your child uses is "scaled down" to his or her size. There is a great deal of evidence that suggests that adult-sized sports implements such as bats, tennis rackets, and basketballs cause children to use modified skills to compensate. They will learn more adult-like skills and be better off in the long run if they use equipment that is proportional to their body size.

One way to check on the appropriateness of the equipment is to watch the motor skill that results when a child uses a particular piece. If golf clubs are too long, they will produce a flatter swing plane than if the clubs are the correct length. Similarly, if a bat or racket is too heavy, a child will "hike" his or her shoulder to gain enough strength to swing it. Watch for these signs to detect problems with the equipment.

You can judge the appropriateness of equipment by asking a few questions:

- Is the equipment of a weight the child can handle?
- Is the equipment of a proportional size for the child?
- Is the equipment safe (shatterproof; splinterproof; guaranteed)?
- Is the equipment endorsed by a sport-governing body?

If you are in doubt about the appropriateness of equipment, check with the local commissioner of a league or the sport-governing body for the particular sport. In addition, though it is no guarantee, if you buy from a reputable sports dealer, you often will receive good advice and be able to purchase quality equipment.

Modify Rules

Rules of the game should also match the size and ability of the participants. Modifying a sport to protect young participants is a simple investment in children's health and enjoyment. Eliminating checking in ice hockey, lowering baskets in basketball, and reducing the size and weight of soccer balls are all examples of rule changes that encourage skill development and reduce the likelihood of injury. Responsible and knowledgeable adults must demand that the competitive rules consider the equipment, dimensions of the playing field, and the length of the contests to protect the young athletes.

You can usually tell easily if rules should be modified for children. When kids leave a contest exhausted or never seem to be able to score points, something must be wrong. Reading children's reactions is the most important way to determine if rules should be altered. For example, when children seem to be bored or listless during a softball game, it may be because they need some new challenges. Consider redefining an "inning" as when everyone bats, or perhaps five children bat. In that way, no one team dominates the play and everyone stays interested. You might also try requiring that each child play at least three different positions, or that in each new game, each child play a new position. If learning to hit and field are primary objectives, perhaps the coach or pitcher of the team at bat should pitch and be charged with delivering the ball over the plate so the children can hit it. After all, isn't that what the game is all about?

The only limitations to creating modified games are those we place on ourselves. Consider the following questions if you're thinking of possible modifications:

- Are there ways in which the scoring of the game could be changed to more closely match the purposes or goals for the children (e.g., improvement vs. winning)?
- Can the scoring be changed to emphasize individual improvement (e.g., unlimited substitutions)?
- Are the dimensions of the playing area appropriate?
- Is the length of the contest appropriate?
- Are the skill requirements too complex? How could the game be simplified?

Many sport-governing bodies have published modified rules for their games. By writing to these agencies or contacting the local parks and recreation department, you may be able to find some creative alternatives to try.

Perhaps the best source of information is the children themselves. Kids are very creative and may have some wonderful ideas. For example, our local soccer league asked the 8-year-old players if they had any thoughts on making the game more fun. They recommended redefining teams as eight players each, having no goalie, and playing across half of the field instead of down the regulation-sized field. These suggestions provided more playing time for everyone, more efficient use of space, and more direct contact with the ball for each participant.

By keeping in mind the maturational level of the children and their goals for participation, you can match the nature of the game with the needs of the children. Don't be afraid to experiment and to ask the children what they think.

Match Developmental Levels

The maturational or developmental level of the children must be considered when you design practice or playing conditions. There are two major issues to consider: matching the competitors against or with each other, and matching the demands of the competition to the participants. There are several important factors to consider when matching the players within groups. In some sports, it is essential to match players on the basis of age or physical size, especially in contact sports such as wrestling or football. For most individual sports, though, matching youngsters in terms of skill level or experience would be most important. To match children most appropriately, consider the following questions:

- How important is size?
- How important is experience or skill levels? If important, consider grouping children based on a skill test or demonstrated proficiency in the activity.
- Is gender a major factor? It usually isn't, except in terms of social expectations, but it is in contact sports after puberty.

Often it is better to group young athletes by skill level and perhaps maturational age rather than the traditional age-only criterion because children of the same age can vary widely in height and weight. A good example of this is the fact that 11-year-olds can vary by as much as 50 pounds in weight and 11 inches in height and still be "average" 11-year-olds.

Grouping children appropriately is particularly important for safety. While the actual risks of injury depend on the sport itself, the level of competition, and the amount of supervision, the group your child competes against may be important to consider. The risks of injury are greater as the degree of physical contact increases or as the differences between athletes increase. If your child is playing with others of similar size and ability, the child will face less risk of injury than if he or she were competing with older, bigger, or more skilled players.

Parents and coaches also can do a lot to help guarantee safe participation in sport by matching practices and competitions to the needs and abilities of the athletes. Careful control of the length and intensity of practices and competitions can help prevent injuries. Sometimes practice sessions last too long, tiring the young athletes unnecessarily, and young tired bodies become more susceptible to injury. Similarly, when intense competition develops, some children take more risks, make poorer judgments, and increase their possibility of injury. Parents and coaches must make the effort to avoid the increased possibility of injury because of fatigue or overly intense competition.

Be Prepared for Emergencies

Sport participation almost always involves some risks and increased chances for injury. Such chances can be reduced by careful precautions. All adults involved in sport should be expected to know basic first aid procedures. Whether the danger is a minor sprain or a serious contact injury, you must be prepared to deal with it. If you are not sure what to do, contact your local American Red Cross for a book on first aid or sign up for an introductory course in first aid techniques. If you are coaching a contact sport or a sport in which an implement is used, it is particularly important for you to know basic first aid.

Collision sports may produce injuries even under the best of conditions. For that reason, many football, lacrosse, and wrestling leagues have begun to require that qualified or trained medical personnel be available at all contests. If this is not the case in your area, be sure that your child's team establishes sound first aid procedures ahead of time.

Emergency plans and safety rules should be designed before the first practice begins. For most team sports, an "informed consent" form and medical clearance should be secured from parents before the season begins. Specific medical procedures should be communicated in writing to parents and players. Such emergency plans should include answers to these questions:

- What is the nearest medical assistance? How can it be contacted?
- Who in the family should be contacted in case of an emergency?
- What medical history is required?
- Where would an injured player be taken in case of an emergency?

These minimal guidelines are essential for all sport participation. No one wants to deal with a serious injury, but it helps to be prepared.

Safe participation in sport will be more likely if precautions are taken ahead of time. Guidelines for safety should be set, including medical examinations, insurance, emergency plans, and general safety rules. Children should be educated about their responsibilities for ensuring safety and about a procedure for contacting you, the parent, in case of a serious injury.

Be Sure the Environment Is Safe

The environment in which a child plays or practices can also be a source of safety hazards. Playing fields, swimming pools, and gymnasia must be inspected before play is allowed. Many playing surfaces are used for multiple purposes, and may contain such dangers as glass, rocks, wire, or even leftover golf balls from someone else's practice!

Broken or dangerous structures should be repaired immediately. A backstop or bleacher with splinters or loose wire can easily snag a young player. Local police departments will also tell you that equipment in disrepair is known to serve as an invitation to vandalism. Therefore, in order to protect both the athletes and the facilities, be sure that potentially dangerous items are inspected and repaired.

Get a Medical Examination for Your Child

Most active, vigorous children are healthy, so the need for medical examinations is often questioned. Pediatricians generally recommend routine physical exams for children and adolescents every 2 or 3 years, with annual checks on vision, hearing, height, weight, and posture.

Since children are generally great barometers of their own health, watch them for cues that medical advice should be sought. For instance, look for changes in regular habits such as sleep patterns, eating preferences or quantities, and consumption of water or other liquids. In addition, specific manifestations such as persistent stiffness and changes in posture, height, or weight may signal potential problems. Be a good observer and encourage your child to tell you how he or she feels. A few aches and pains are normal, but persistent ones should be checked by a physician.

As your child chooses to participate in higher levels of competition, his or her behavior may become less reliable as a barometer to health. At higher levels, children become more intense, others pressure them to play, and the value of playing may override their feelings of pain or fatigue. Because of these conditions, medical examinations are generally valuable safety precautions.

Special Hazards of Strenuous Activity

Young children are quite resilient to physical stress. Their heart and lungs are designed to support their energy needs in exercise. However, the human body is like a fine machine, and it must be treated properly. There are some physical stresses in sport to which young children are particularly susceptible, such as effects on skeletal bone formation and growth patterns and responses to heat and dehydration.

Stress to Bones

In children, the bones are often the first part of the body to react to stress. The immature skeleton can be seriously injured if stress is unreasonably imposed or if symptoms of injury are ignored. Symptoms generally include pain, tenderness, or reduced ability to move through the total range of motion.

Children grow because of growth plates near the ends of their bones. These centers of growth are made of soft cartilage and are responsible for allowing the bone to continue to grow. The growth plates in the long bones of the arms and legs are areas where young athletes are prone to injury. When a child reaches mature adult height, these growth plates disappear, thus stopping further growth. However, an injury before full maturity can interrupt normal growth patterns. A serious growth plate injury in a 14-year-old could cause a loss of a quarter-inch in height, while the same injury in a 7-year-old could cause a 4- or 5-inch deficit. However, if training is of moderate intensity, and if the early signs of injury are heeded and appropriate medical attention is obtained, potential long-term damage can be avoided.

Activities that place heavy stress on one body part are particularly dangerous in children. The "Little Leaguer's elbow" is an example of how repeated, powerful throws can place stress on the elbow of the throwing arm. Sport rules often restrict pitchers to six innings per week or three innings in 3 days so boys and girls will not unduly stress their arms. These rules are very important to the safety of young baseball pitchers. Since the rules were introduced, less than 2% of the pitchers have sustained arm injuries. When injuries do occur, a rest period (sometimes as long as 6 months) will normally eliminate the problem. Rule changes such as these can help, but children often want to develop sophisticated skills early. This desire may lead them to continue to throw hard or to try to learn a curve ball even when it is not safe. So beware! You must help them take responsibility for their own safety.

Extensive weight-bearing activities may also cause problems. Activities that are conducted on hard surfaces or produce full extension of the knees or hips can be damaging. Collision sports can produce irreparable damage and should be carefully monitored in young children. Similarly, long-distance running such as marathons on hard roads should be carefully monitored in children. The American Academy of Pediatrics suggests that children under the age of 10 not be allowed to compete at such distances.

Changes in Growth Patterns

Extremely strenuous activity may also have an effect on body growth and maturation patterns. Disruption of normal secondary sex characteristics is a potential concern. For females, it is often evidenced by missed menstrual cycles. This absence of menstruation, athletic amenorrhea, is a normal reaction to stress that occurs in response to vigorous athletic training. It will generally correct itself when stress is reduced. At a recent state high school championship, approximately 50% of the long-distance runners had not menstruated during the previous three months, the time during which they were training strenuously. However, when severe stress was removed, their menstrual cycles returned.

Most pediatricians believe that adolescent female athletes will merely experience irregular menstrual periods. Similarly, the hormonal effect of stress is not fully understood as it affects adolescent males. Neither of these concerns is a reason to limit participation.

Some other physiological changes associated with strenuous activity are brought on by specific behaviors that could be avoided. For example, some young people who practice exaggerated weight control techniques may experience growth retardation. Wrestlers or gymnasts who attempt to change their weight through the use of diuretics or dehydration are a prime example. A philosophy of moderation would produce much healthier athletes. There should be no need for young males and females to purge their bodies to maintain weight standards. Careful monitoring of diet will help them develop as stronger and healthier individuals.

Heat Sensitivity

The human body responds to heat by sweating and increased blood flow to the skin. This increased blood flow allows the blood to cool because of the evaporation of sweat on the skin. In heavy exercise, heat is released by both conduction and radiation, as well as through breathing and sweating. The red-faced child is showing good adjustment to heat. This thermoregulation is one of the most important safety features of the human body.

When the weather is hot and dry, heat loss occurs primarily through sweating and the evaporation of moisture from the skin. The fluids lost through sweating must be replaced! The best plan to protect your athlete from heat illness is to have liquids available at all times. Young athletes should be encouraged to drink small amounts often, and in no case should they be deprived of fluids as a motivator or punishment. Encourage them to drink!

Many commercial fluid products are available for athletes, but water is the most important fluid to consume. In fact, some experts suggest that the use of special fluids may quench thirst before the real physiological need for fluid is satisfied. For this reason, water still remains the number one drink for athletes!

Many adults grew up in the day of salt tablets. These supplements were once thought to help the body retain liquid but for most healthy eaters, additional salt requires the individual to drink even more water. Salt tablets are not recommended for most young athletes.

The best protection against overheating is to use common sense when practicing and playing. Schedule activity during the cool of the day, rather than at midday. Take breaks often and keep practices short. Keep plenty of fluids on hand. When children play in the sun, have them keep their clothing on, and damp if possible, to aid evaporation and therefore cooling. Such simple tips will have a major impact on the body's ability to accommodate heat.

Summary

The dangers of serious injury in sport are real. But what are the real chances of injury compared to the real benefits of participation? Some of the data may surprise you. Statistics show less chance of being injured while playing ice hockey than while skateboarding; less danger from wrestling than horseback riding; less danger from playing basketball than riding bicycles; and less danger from playing football than from riding in a car. Risks are indeed a part of sport, but not an unusual aspect. Teaching children to be safety conscious and to participate at healthy levels is the key.

Parents and other interested adults have a special responsibility in preventing injuries. Ensuring that your child has adequate strength and flexibility is only one aspect. You must also evaluate the entire sport experience: equipment, rules, developmental levels, emergency preparedness, safe play environments, and medical screening.

You should also understand the special hazards of strenuous activity. Children are generally quite resilient, but there are limits. Monitor normal growth and development in order to detect any unusual hormonal or orthopedic changes in serious young athletes. Such changes are certainly the exception, but concerned parents must be observant ones!

The Importance of Nutrition

Chapter 12

One of the most important elements in the development and nurturing of a child athlete is also one of the most difficult to handle—providing for nutritional needs. Why should this be so? There are several reasons. One is the time element. Practices, travel schedules, and tournaments all seem to disrupt the family meal. Wouldn't it be wonderful if your child said, "I'll be home for lunch today, because practice isn't until 2:30." More typically, your child informs you that he or she won't be home for a prepared meal tonight (or almost any night) by telling you "Coach says we're going to begin practice later this season, so I won't be home until 7:30. I'll stop at Burger Heaven on the way home." Making sure your child athlete gets a balanced diet is sometimes almost impossible, considering after school, Saturday morning, early morning, and evening practices and the fast-food existence such a schedule suggests. If you are the chauffeur, sometimes it's also impossible to make sure the rest of the family eats a balanced diet.

Another reason some child athletes don't eat well is that parents sometimes don't have an adequate understanding of nutrition. What do growing youngsters need? Do all children need the same things, or do budding athletes need different foods? There are many serious misunderstandings about what the best diets are for children in particular sports. For instance, do you know if swimmers should eat differently than cross-country runners or wrestlers? Should boys eat differently than girls? Read on, and we'll discuss these questions.

Components of Good Nutrition

We sometimes hold a misconception about why we eat. Most people think that food is eaten to supply the energy necessary for daily living and exercise. This is true to a certain extent, but calories are only one reason we eat. We also eat to obtain the elements from which our bodies are constructed, such as calcium for bone and protein for muscle. Young growing athletes need food for both reasons, which makes good nutrition even more important for them. It sometimes helps to think of food not as pickles, hamburger, or corn, but as protein, carbohydrate, and fat. Food has six vital components; without the proper quantities of each, your child will not perform to the best of his or her abilities and may not be as healthy as he or she could be. These six components are protein, carbohydrate, fat, vitamins, minerals, and water. Your child must eat foods that contain adequate amounts of each of these nutrients to permit growth and repair and to supply energy for the body.

Protein is necessary for growth and repair. Although protein does provide calories, it should not be considered a major source of calories in your child's diet. Protein is necessary for the development of muscle and for the internal structure of bone. Protein is also an essential part of each cell of the body. If it is used for energy, it will not be available for growth and repair—and there is no substitute for protein. Don't worry, though. Most children in the U.S. eat more than enough protein. As a matter of fact, they probably eat more than they need.

Carbohydrates have one very important role: to supply energy. Some of the energy is used right after eating. Any energy derived from carbohydrates that is not used immediately is stored as glycogen in muscle and liver or changed to fat and stored in the fat cells.

One nice thing about carbohydrates (e.g., potatoes, spaghetti, bread) is that they are good, cheap, and filling for your young "bottomless pit." Carbohydrates are also especially important in long-lasting, high-energy utilizing sports such as long-distance swimming, cycling, and running.

Fat in the diet provides a concentrated energy source. Each ounce of fat contains more than twice as many calories as each ounce of protein or carbohydrate. A child who loses weight because of the heavy energy expenditure in competition may need to include more fat in his or her diet, whereas the child who has a weight problem may need to reduce the amount of fat intake in his or her diet.

Vitamins and minerals don't provide energy per se, but the body doesn't work without them. Vitamins and minerals are essential for muscles, nerves, and brains to work. All the energy will be worthless if your child doesn't have the vitamins and minerals to power the cells. The young athlete needs to know that it is the carrots and broccoli that sharpen reflexes, not the cheeseburgers.

Water is such a critical element for human survival that we sometimes forget to mention it on our list of necessary nutrients. And it's dehydration, the lack of adequate water, that causes most of the immediate nutrition-related problems associated with athletic performance such as fatigue. Make sure your active youngsters drink more than enough liquids. Water is the best choice.

Short of becoming a nutritionist, how can you make sure that your child athlete eats a balanced meal? The easiest way is to teach your child about the food groups. The four food groups described by the federal government—milk, meat, fruit and vegetable, and grain—have been designed to include certain nutrients in each category. This means that your child will have a good probability of eating a balanced diet if we follow the food group plan. Children who consume at least the minimal number of servings each day from the four food groups will usually eat well enough for maximum performance. For children, the minimum number of servings is three to four from the dairy group, two from the meat group, four from the fruit and vegetable group, and four from the grain group. Table 3 shows some selected foods from each food group and their serving sizes.

You should make sure your child is as familiar with the food group plan as you are, because there may be many times the young athlete will have to select his or her own food while traveling. The child also should begin accepting responsibility for the nutritional aspect of his or her athletic career.

Table 3   Examples From the Four Food Groups

Food Group	Serving Size

I. Milk Group (4)*		**III. Fruit/Vegetable Group (4)***	
Milks	8 oz	Cooked fruit	½ c
Yogurt	8 oz	Fruit juice	½ c
Cheese	1½ oz	Medium-size fruit	1
Ice cream	1¾ c	Cooked vegetables	½ c
Cottage cheese	2 c	Raw vegetables	1 c
Pudding	1 c		
Chowder	1 c		
II. Meat Group (2)*		**IV. Grain Group (4)***	
Meats	2 oz.	Bread	1 slice
Fish	2 oz	Ready-to-eat cereals	1 c
Poultry	2 oz	Cooked cereals	½ c
Cheese	2 oz	Spaghetti, noodles	½ c
Eggs	2	Pancakes, waffles	1
Cottage cheese	½ c		
Dried peas, beans	1 c		
Peanut butter	4 tbsp		
Nuts	½-1 c		

*Servings per day.

Supplements

Many erroneous ideas have arisen about nutrition for athletes. One of the most persistent is the idea that athletes need to supplement their diets, either with vitamins or protein.

Vitamin Supplements

Many parents ask if their children should take vitamin supplements, especially parents who want to make sure that their child has the best shot at high-level athletic performance. There is no one answer for every child. If your child has terrible nutritional habits, vitamin supplements may not be able to make up the deficiency anyway. Perhaps the best advice is to make sure that your child is eating a balanced diet when at home, and that he or she tries to eat well during the season. Vitamin supplements should only be necessary when it is difficult or impossible for the child to eat a balanced diet.

Megavitamins are not needed under any circumstances. Select a multivitamin and mineral complex that meets 100% of the daily needs of your diet and have the child use it as a second choice to a good diet.

Protein Supplementation

The need for protein supplementation is one of the major myths associated with athletic performance. Some athletes who desire large muscles for their sport such as football players and weight lifters are convinced they need to supplement their already hefty protein intake with protein powders and drinks. The body can only use so much protein, and the muscles increase in size in response to the work they are asked to do, not to the amount of protein ingested. Extra protein will not make the muscles increase in size any faster. You need to make sure that your child has an adequate, but not excessive, amount of protein in his diet. Use the guidelines in the food group plan. Anything more is simply expensive calories. Sure, some football players do eat 10 steaks and 3 dozen eggs for breakfast, and they are big and strong. But other football players are vegetarians, and they are just as big and strong. Advise your growing athlete to eat a healthy, balanced diet and to skip the protein powders. Excessive protein consumption can cause dehydration, and the first sign of dehydration is fatigue—just what the athlete wants to avoid.

Competition and Nutrition

Many questions arise about eating and competition. How can your child eat well while he or she is on the go? What should he or she eat just before competing—or during a competition? And how important is it to drink enough water during and after competing?

Eating on the Road

Unless you follow your child around the tournament trail in a motorized van with a built-in kitchen, you're not going to be able to control his or her diet. Nor should you. Children should begin taking responsibility for following the food group plan when they are away from home. But what if fast food restaurants are the only choice? A few rules might help.

- Drink milk rather than soft drinks. Milk provides vitamins A and D, protein, and calcium. (Note that most "shakes" do not contain any milk!)
- Choose fish sandwiches rather than fried or grilled hamburgers. Fish sandwiches are healthier because they usually have less grease, and the stomach won't be as likely to be upset before a big match.
- Go to places that have a salad bar, potatoes, or spaghetti. Carbohydrates are a healthy source of nutrition without the problems of high fat or calories. They should be a large portion of the food consumed during competition and especially when traveling. Carbohydrates provide the most efficient source of fuel available to the body. In contrast, fatty foods take longer to digest so the time between eating and playing must be longer if the athlete is to avoid the sensation of "a rock in the stomach."
- Skip the sweets as much as possible. Spaghetti would make a better snack than a candy bar. Eating too many sweets will produce a tremendous variation in a person's blood glucose level, and may severely affect the energy level of an athlete during competition. Sweets tend to produce a quick "energy high" that may suddenly end in the middle of a game. In addition the long-term effects of eating sweets to satisfy hunger can only lead to a lack of adequate nutrition and potential weight problems.

Pregame Meals

There are many superstitions surrounding the pregame meal. For most athletes, the benefits of a pregame meal are more psychological than physical. In fact, eating before competition often has a negative effect, except in the case of marathon or all-day competitions.

The current knowledge regarding pregame meals emphasizes three points:

- *The pregame meal by itself cannot produce a superior performance.* However, it can negatively affect performance. Eating right before a performance cannot add strength or skill, but instead may cause a child's physiological system to divert needed blood from the muscles to the stomach. Three hours before competition is usually the best time for a meal.

- *It is better to eat too little than too much.* It takes about 3 hours to empty the stomach. For individuals who suffer from anxiety or indigestion, eating a substantial amount right before a performance can cause problems.
- *If a pregame meal is important, eat foods that are digested easily.* Some young athletes need food for physical or psychological reasons. Feeling hungry is typical for many adolescents, especially young athletes. If so, let them eat carbohydrates, not fats. Focus on easily digested foods, not the high-fat meals.

If your child wishes to eat before performing, there are three factors to keep in mind about the precompetition meal. One is the placebo, or psychological, effect of food, the factor you're probably most familiar with. The child from the next town who beats your child regularly always eats a candy bar exactly 1 hour before the match, so that's what your child "must" eat. Many young athletes develop eating habits that border on superstitions. A local junior tennis star insists that a "Big Mac" an hour before play is critical to her success. The nutritional value of the food is much less important than its value as a placebo for her. Given her past experience and reliance on this particular type of food, she might lose if she didn't eat one an hour before the match. And that's fine, as long as eating that much doesn't interfere with her performance during the match.

A second factor to consider in the precompetition meal is the "butterfly" factor. If your child's anxiety is manifested through his or her stomach, it is probably better for the young athlete to eat foods that are easy to digest, have little fat in them, and/or are liquid rather than solid. Foods such as spaghetti, that don't have a lot of fat in them, should be selected for a pregame meal. If the athlete has a high butterfly factor, a real milk shake or orange juice may be better.

The third factor to consider is the length of the competitive event. For example, the 100-meter dash is over in a matter of seconds, but the high-jump competition may last most of the day before a winner is determined. Cross-country meets may take minutes, whereas marathons last for several hours. The longer the event will last, the more important it is for your child to eat a substantive precompetition meal.

There is no magic about nutrition. If you can help your child understand its important role in fueling the body, he or she will make better choices about what and when he or she eats.

Eating During Competition

Many young athletes like to eat while they compete, especially in activities where there are time delays or breaks in the action. One father recently asked, "My son insists on taking a peanut butter and jelly sandwich to eat between innings of his baseball games. Sometimes he even eats a hot dog or ice cream sandwich. Does he really need that much food?" The answer is yes and no. Yes, he probably does need that much food each day, because he may be growing at a fast rate. But no, he probably doesn't need it during the baseball game, at least not for calories—but have you asked him if the stickiness helps him get a good grip on the bat or if the food just makes him feel like playing baseball?

Some types of competition involve the hurry-up-and-wait approach to sport. There may be long breaks between events, especially during tournaments (baseball, tennis) or meets (swimming, track and field, gymnastics). In meets or tournaments where the breaks are 40 minutes or longer, it may be to your child's advantage to eat small snacks. Good choices are milk, cheese, peanut butter, juices, and light sandwiches. This food is easily digested and does not place an undue demand on the body's digestive system. In addition, foods with protein in them such as cheese, milk, or peanuts are more slowly broken down into sources of glucose and produce a more sustained source of energy than typical simple sugar sources such as candy bars.

Water and Dehydration

Replacing energy that has been used with food is important, but the most important thing to replace during competition is water. Your child must have plenty of water during competition, especially during hot or humid weather, for two very important reasons. First, it is dangerous to compete when dehydrated. Heat exhaustion or heat stroke can occur, with sometimes fatal consequences. In heat exhaustion, the athlete feels temporarily exhausted and may complain of headaches or nausea. The best remedy is to get out of the sun, rest, and cool off in the shower while replenishing liquids. Heat stroke, a much more serious condition, occurs when the regulatory system of the body fails, producing vascular complications. The symptoms may involve high fever, rapid pulse, and loss of awareness or even loss of consciousness. This condition should be treated with immediate actions to reduce the body heat by seeking shade, applying cold towels, and sending for emergency medical assistance. The best prevention for excess heat is to drink liquids.

The second reason a fluid balance is essential is that performance can be significantly affected by inadequate fluid intake. The first sign of dehydration is fatigue. Tell your child to drink liquids even though he or she may not be thirsty. The thirst mechanism doesn't always keep up with water needs during heavy physical activity. Always replace a day's weight loss with water.

Weight Loss in Athletes

The control of weight is important in all athletic activities. The human body functions best when there is an optimal relationship between muscle (lean mass) and energy sources (fats and carbohydrates). Our bodies also require other nutrients in order to maximize performance.

Making Weight

In sport, there are many times when being thin can be to your advantage. Competition in some sports is divided by weight classes, especially in youth sport, boxing, and wrestling. This may encourage some athletes, especially wrestlers, to keep their weight too low or to try to "make weight" or change weight classes through rapid weight loss.

Remember that the first sign of dehydration is fatigue. Wrestlers get fooled thinking that dropping down a weight class will win them the championship, although they may actually win because they are wrestling against another athlete who is just as fatigued from dehydration. Rapid weight loss is unhealthy and can only interfere with optimal performance. You may wish to consider whether it is better for your child to attempt to lose the weight or to remain in his natural weight class.

If your child honestly needs to lose excess weight, a sensible long-term effort should be undertaken. If the child is exercising extensively each day, then moderate caloric reduction is the option to choose. Limit the weight loss to 1 to 1.5 pounds per week. A rule of thumb is that a total reduction of 3,500 calories will result in a loss of 1 pound per week. The first step is to reduce the amount of fat in the diet, because it contains more than twice as many calories per ounce as the other types of food.

Reducing the fat in one's diet is healthy not only for weight control but also for general health. For example, a baked potato contains

90 calories, but a French fried potato contains more than double the calories with no increase in nutritional value.

One of the problems children can develop when trying to lose weight is getting into a cycle of being tempted to eat, eating, and then regretting it. They sometimes cope with this cycle by inducing vomiting or taking laxatives. The practice of inducing vomiting, however, is not a healthy substitute for careful eating. It can have serious physical and psychological side effects and should not be encouraged. Some evidence now indicates that incidental, voluntarily induced vomiting may lead to the serious psychological problem of bulimia discussed in the next section.

If your child needs to lose weight and is not fatigued from sport practice, a combination of more exercise and less food intake is the best choice. Children who compete seasonally may have difficulty with a weight gain in the off-season if they maintain their same food intake with a reduced energy expenditure. Awareness of this possibility along with good eating habits combats the problem.

Eating Disorders: Anorexia and Bulimia

Young people in today's culture seem to place an inordinate value on thinness. Though it is true that relatively low amounts of fat are good, there are optimal levels. For most athletes the percentage of fat to total body mass should be about 8-12% fat for males and 16-20% for females.

As some young people become conscious of their weight and strive for optimal leanness, they overreact and become too thin. When the desire to be thin becomes compulsive and interferes with normal or regular eating habits, these youngsters may have a serious psychological problem.

For some young people, the compulsive desire to be thin results in a complete lack of appetite and unrealistic body perception. A psychological state of anorexia may develop in which the individual, often an adolescent female, refuses to eat. This produces a vicious cycle of lost weight, lost appetite, and low self-concept.

Anorexia is a serious psychological illness that must be treated with professional counseling. It can lead to permanent health problems and, in extreme cases, even death. There are, however, many successful treatment strategies available today, and these should be pursued at the first sign of a potential eating problem.

The second form of eating disorder, bulimia, results when an individual has severe guilt after eating. The guilt may lead to vomiting and consequent loss of nutrition. Many individuals who feel a loss of control while eating compensate for it by intentionally inducing vomiting to purge the food.

Bulimia is also a very serious condition. A bulimic child is sometimes hard to detect because such a child appears to have a good appetite, even an excessive one. The act of vomiting is often hidden from parents or friends. In fact, parents of bulimic children sometimes have mentioned that they thought their children were the lucky ones with "high metabolisms"; they seemed to be able to eat anything without gaining any weight. Be on the alert for such symptoms in your child and seek help as soon as you become concerned.

Nutritional Role Models

All of us tend to pattern ourselves after someone. We may dress like someone, or talk like someone, or hit a tennis serve like someone we admire. You may also find that your child athlete wants to eat like his or her favorite sport star. This is fine as long as the role model has sensible eating habits. But many of the professional athletes eat unhealthy foods, or say they do for publicity's sake. Football players eating raw eggs and raw meat are frequently reported. Neither is good for the pro player or for your child. Raw eggs can interfere with the absorption of vitamins, and raw meat can give you trichinosis (beef as well as pork). Help your child find a sensible role model and learn to use the food group plan for nutritional success.

Summary

The human body can only function as well as it is fed. Eating properly will not improve skills, but it will allow the execution of skills that have been practiced and learned. Young athletes must understand the importance of nutrition and learn to eat responsibly. If you expect your child to take responsibility for regular practice, include nutrition as part of those practice goals. Food is not a miracle drug, but it is an absolute necessity for optimal performance.

Under most circumstances, proper nutrition can be maintained by eating the recommended number of daily servings from each of the four food groups: milk and milk products, three to four; meat, poultry, and fish, two; fruits and vegetables, four; grains, four. If each of these group requirements is met, no supplemental sources are required. Competing in sport sometimes means your child doesn't have access to the right kinds of food. Make sure you educate him or her about the best eating choices while on the road and during competition. Discourage your child from attempting to lose weight too quickly. It can injure your child's health and may lead to more serious eating disorders. Remember—if we are what we eat, then your child must eat right to perform at his or her best.

Section III

Sport as a
Total Experience

This section emphasizes the total experience of sport. It begins with a discussion of the nature of the sport experience for children. How can sport contribute to the development of each child? Do all sports need to be modeled after professional sport? How can children be challenged and not threatened by competition?

The benefits of sport participation and its contribution to total development are discussed in the next chapter, including the relationship between sport achievement and personal and academic achievement. Does sport really build character? Is there a future benefit for your child? How can athletics and academics be balanced? Who determines the value of sport and the values transmitted and developed in sport?

Understanding your child's growth as a person in general and in sport in particular is the focus of the final chapter. Many questions from other parents are presented and suggestions are provided for their resolution. Some final thoughts about being a parent are presented, including a code of ethics to use as a guide to dealing with future problems and possibilities.

Organized Youth Sport: Can It Be for All?

Chapter 13

Organized sport such as Little League-type baseball, football, or soccer, bowling leagues, and junior tennis or golf leagues has many positive influences on children. A well-organized, well-led sport program can help teach many things. Organized sport participation can encourage values such as teamwork, following orders, obeying rules, achievement, and the pleasure of challenging oneself that are important to each person.

In addition to these league-type opportunities, there are many competitive agency sport programs. Children who travel and compete independently learn many valuable lessons and personal skills.

Youth sport programs have grown tremendously in the past 20 years. They represent a major source of leisure time activity for both children and adults. However, the role of youth sport must focus on the child, not the needs of the adult organizers, sponsors, coaches, or parents.

Participation for All

Organized youth sport teams should ensure participation for all. A recent survey of over 1,000 participants in Little League baseball showed that among those teams that did not finish first in their leagues, most boys and girls indicated they would much rather play on a losing team than sit on the bench for a winner. This feeling was especially true of younger children, while older athletes tended to reduce their own desire to participate in favor of a more team-oriented goal.

Many attempts have been made in recent years to encourage sport participation for all children. The equal-time or minimum inning rules in baseball, for instance, were introduced to foster the skill development of each child. In theory they were great ideas, but in practice they often worked to the detriment of some children.

Sometimes the embarrassment or resentment felt by a child who knows the coach must play him or her will overshadow any positive effects of participation. For example, some baseball leagues have the three-inning minimum rule. This concept was introduced as a way to allow all children the experience of competition. It does that, but what else does it do?

A recent game may serve as an excellent example. The Sox were leading the Cardinals by six runs when the coach realized his three "motor morons" were still on the bench. Knowing the rules, he introduced each one into the batting order, and subsequently into right field, catching, and third base. Unfortunately, the three young players, known as "Butterfingers Bobbie," "Silly Cid," and "Slowpoke Sam," committed nine errors between them and the Sox lost the game. Of what value was the minimum inning rule for these three young athletes? It probably only reinforced their already low self-concepts, the negative feelings directed toward them by their teammates, and the overall loss for the team. In this case, the coach probably did not use good judgment in employing the rule change. The rule was intended to help the children gain experience, not to embarrass them.

The concept of participation for all is obviously a desired goal. But there are other rule changes that could accomplish this without hurting either the less talented players or the team. For instance, why not couple the three-inning rule with unrestricted substitutions? In this way, players could be moved in and out of the game, and could have the benefit of game experience with much less peer pressure. The three players in the previous example could play in any one inning, rotate in and out, and not feel directly responsible for a negative outcome. Other players could reenter the game at crucial moments.

Such sensible rule changes can be applied to widen access to many sports. A youth sports program in Washington has adopted rule changes in softball that promote skill development, teamwork, and sportsmanship. All players who come to a game must be listed in the batting order and must bat before any other player can bat a second time, though the specific order can change throughout the game. Innings are defined as nine batters, players can alternate positions in the field, and must bat whether they are actually playing in the field or not. All players play an equal amount during each game and in some leagues the pitchers pitch to their own teammates—after all, the idea is to hit, run, and field. As the children advance in age or ability, the rules become more consistent with adult sport programs.

Other rule changes may include having players experience a variety of positions. In baseball, some leagues allow children to practice and play one position for a week and then rotate to a different position. As a result, all children get an opportunity to experience and develop the skills necessary to play all positions.

Scoring rules can also increase the benefits of sport participation. In basketball, if one team gets ahead by 20 points in the second half, that team can be declared the winner or the composition of teams can change. But the game would continue with all reserves playing. This rule emphasizes participation and prevents one team from getting "creamed."

Just as rule changes can give all children a chance to participate and enjoy sport, physical modifications to games can promote participation. Often, however, there is opposition to such changes. Most children enjoy being like "real athletes," and most adults share their belief that only adult rules are acceptable. Modified games are sometimes seen as less desirable, perhaps as not using all the same skills needed for playing a "real" game. Some parents and coaches argue that modified sports will retard the skill development of the most talented children.

But these objections don't hold up when we look at the facts. First, it is obvious that children and adults are quite different in size. Because the size of a participant is directly related to his or her ability to run fast, throw, kick, strike, and catch large objects, it seems only reasonable to scale down the physical aspects of sports to fit children. Field and court sizes can and should be reduced so the distances are more reasonable. Smaller or lighter balls, bats, and rackets can be used to encourage good skill development and increase the chances of success.

Basketball gives us a good example. The average adult male basketball player can spread his hand 8.75 inches from the thumb to the tip of his little finger, or about 28.7% of the circumference of a regulation basketball. When this same basketball is used by 9- to 13-year-olds, whose hands spread only about 7.5 inches, or 25% of the circumference of the ball, it is obvious that the young athlete is at a decided disadvantage. This unequal size problem could be reduced by using a "junior-sized" basketball that is 2 inches smaller in circumference.

The advantage of playing under more reasonable conditions becomes even more important when we realize that it contributes to better skill learning. Most research and practical evidence indicate that children must learn games skills before they can ever excel. Playing with smaller equipment on smaller fields allows children to become more proficient at game skills. They then can adjust to "real-life" size as their own bodies grow and mature. Such modifications make the game more enjoyable and motivating.

The child who has "star" potential can be encouraged and allowed to advance to other areas of competition with more traditional equipment or rules as he or she becomes more proficient. In the meantime, the child will benefit by mastering skills correctly in the modified game. If children's needs and abilities are kept in mind, modifying rules can help all young athletes.

Youth sports should be administered with a child's eye view. When games are created from this point of view, they are generally appropriate and positive experiences for children. Games must be matched to the athletes' abilities, skills, and needs. Young children themselves often suggest the length of games should be cut, the size of the field or goals reduced, and the time spent on the bench lessened!

For instance, one neighborhood group was recently observed setting up a pick-up hockey game. The players agreed that there should be no slap shots. The rule protected them because most were not wearing pads, and also made the play more equal because some of the skaters did not have well-developed slap shots.

Another example of children modifying their own rules occurred in a football league in Illinois. Each child was asked to identify what he or she thought were the most important skills in football. The children voted that throwing and catching were the most important skills, followed by running with the ball. When asked what changes they would make in the present league rules, they decided on an unlimited number of hand-offs and forward passes. This new style of football, called "razzle-dazzle football," has provided for more skill development with fewer injuries and much more involvement and fun.

Direct Versus Indirect Competition

As previously mentioned, a potential weakness in most American sport is that it produces more losers than winners. But today many adults are succeeding at helping young athletes strive to do their best, to improve upon their previous best performances, to pursue their own personal level of excellence, and to redefine success. This approach allows athletes to strive to attain their potential and reduces the anxieties associated with constant comparisons to others.

Competitive situations can be created in which each child is judged by how much improvement has been made, not by whether he or she won or lost. One local swim league recently instituted a new set of competitive rules. League officials decided that the important part of competition was to encourage children to do better each time they participated. Improvement was hard to measure, however, when success was only judged in terms of each swimmer's wins and losses, so at the regular swimming meets, officials instituted a new team scoring system. Each swimmer submitted his or her best three times for each event in the preseason meets. These times became the standard for that individual swimmer, and scoring in the swim meet was based on whether the swimmer improved on that time. Two points were awarded if a swimmer's time was at least 2% better than his or her previous average. If a swimmer did about the same (plus or minus 2% of the average), he or she earned 1 point for the team. If a swimmer did not match the average (minus 3% or more), he or she did not contribute any points to the team total. Each week a new target time was calculated for each swimmer. The standard of success was therefore adjusted for the individual and his or her own progress.

At the end of the swimming season, all swimmers were asked to evaluate the system. Over 90% of the swimmers thought this was a better way to judge swimming meets. The 10% who did not support the handicap system were generally the better swimmers who had already been "winning" and for whom a little improvement was more difficult to achieve. The children felt this system was a good way for them to measure their own success and progress. Unfortunately, almost 80% of the parents did not like the system, because it did not provide them with a good measure of whether their child or their child's team was "better" than someone else.

This type of indirect competition can be a positive experience for all children. They are not forced to compete directly against each other because every competitor could be a winner (or loser). Indirect competition can be an experience in which young athletes strive to do their individual bests and learn to be controlled by internal rather than external capabilities and expectations.

Children seek many ways in which they can measure their sport competence. These experiences may involve personal challenges and do not always require interpersonal challenges where someone wins at the expense of others. Unfortunately, as children grow older, direct personal confrontations tend to become more prevalent and may threaten not only their skill development but their personal self esteem. At some point all athletes seek to measure their skill against others, but that does not need to be the only measuring stick.

As competition between players becomes more direct, the "stakes" of the competition also become higher. The personal gains that are possible through sport and competition can have both positive and negative effects on children. The nature or structure of the games does not necessarily change, but the ways in which children participate change markedly. The interaction between players becomes more forceful as their intentions become more serious. The simple tag games of childhood become much different as they evolve into ball tag, bombardment, lacrosse, soccer, or football.

Parents who focus on helping their children learn good skills will establish the foundation for maintaining interest during later years. Children seek to learn, perform, and improve. They like to be good at what they do and to be able to display their skills. Their attention spans will lengthen and they will focus on specific goals and skills if they remain interested.

Children vary tremendously both in ability and interest. The earlier suggestions that you must treat each child as a unique individual and provide both direct and indirect competition are true for all children, but especially for teens and preteens. There are children at age 13 who win gold medals (Tracy Caulkins, Pan Am swimmer from Maryland) or U.S. Open Tennis Titles (Tracy Austin) while others are doing a front dive or holding a tennis racket for the first time in their lives!

As a parent you must learn to meet your child at his or her level and to establish challenging and meaningful experiences. You will need a keen mind and a creative sense to set goals that will challenge your child to strive just beyond present capabilities but are not so unrealistic as to frustrate or discourage participation. Perhaps the adage that we should "attempt to reach just beyond our grasp" provides a good reminder of the need to constantly try to improve ourselves and not be satisfied with the present status. This is an important point to emphasize to your child as he or she strives to improve.

Summary

The value of sport participation lies in its potential to allow each child to be challenged and to strive to improve. Sport participation also provides an opportunity to measure one's own ability in terms of past capacity and in relation to others. Sport experiences can be structured in terms of the needs and abilities of the children involved. Games should be modified to meet the objectives of competition. Rule changes can enhance the pleasure and goal accomplishment for each child. As the child's abilities increase, the nature of the challenge can become more difficult or more traditional. The key is to match the experience with the capabilities and needs of each child.

The Benefits
of Sport Participation

Chapter 14

This chapter, rather than focusing on how to develop a child athlete, will focus on why to develop a child athlete. Although there are skeptics, most people agree that sport can be an excellent training ground for developing qualities, abilities, and attitudes that form adults who are able to function effectively in a competitive society.

Sport supporters argue that a commitment to sport can successfully foster higher educational aspirations, lead to the development of necessary social skills, teach a process useful in later life, support moral beliefs acceptable in society, and lead to enhanced self-esteem. Let's take a closer look at the benefits supposedly derived from sport participation to appreciate the reasons sport might be a valuable experience for your child.

Sport and Education

Although athletics and education sometimes seem to be in opposition, your child's participation in sport can actually help him or her achieve academic success. It can also encourage him or her to go on to higher education. If so, you and your child need to choose a school carefully to ensure a first-rate education as well as first-rate sport opportunities.

Athletic Participation and Academic Achievement

Is sport participation really of value to the immediate- and long-range happiness and success of your child? Should you encourage your child to strive to be the best that he or she can be in both sport and school?

You should encourage your child to do the best at whatever he or she chooses. Because all children in America must attend school, to some extent you must encourage good school performance. You should encourage your child to strive to the best of his or her abilities in scholastic endeavors, but the best opportunities in life often go to true scholar athletes. For example, many individuals in managerial positions or those responsible for hiring in businesses suggest that the most desirable applicants for jobs are individuals categorized as former scholar athletes.

Research studies designed to answer this question have consistently shown that in general athletes get better grades than non-athletes. The difference in grades is most dramatic for children from low- or middle-socioeconomic families. Children in these groups who are athletes tend to get better grades than children who are not athletes. This means that sport may be most beneficial to academic performance for those children who are most likely to be frustrated and perform poorly in school.

Many factors may influence athletes to do better in school. Athletes often experience special pressures to perform well in the classroom because they need to retain academic eligibility to participate. This is obviously important for all school sports, since there are minimum eligibility requirements in every state. The best student athletes also feel the pressure and competition for a college or university scholarship.

Athletes are frequently given extra attention and encouragement to do well in school because of these pressures and the value placed on athletic participation. The special help athletes receive from teachers, peers, and coaches can have a profound effect on scholastic attainment.

Because athletes have limited free time because of practices and training schedules, they must learn to use their time efficiently and plan for specific study periods. This encourages or forces athletes to learn to organize time and space for maximum benefit. Many successful businessmen have reported that learning to set priorities and managing time were two of the most important lessons learned from sport.

The differences between athletes and nonathletes do not stop here, but often these effects only occur because athletes wish to be able to play in college. Parents concerned about their child truly getting a quality education will have to place special emphasis on academics and make such performance a requirement for sport involvement. Athletes are found to have higher educational goals and actually attain higher levels of education than nonathletes.

The self-esteem and confidence gained from athletics can spill over into academic areas and improve the athlete's motivation for excellence in education. Likewise, the important sporting values of working hard, persistence, and believing in one's ability may carry over to academic endeavors.

Some schools reward athletics and academics differently. The most desirable school might well be one in which individuals were rewarded only when both academic and athletic achievement or improvement are present. Such an environment would maintain a positive relationship between athletic participation and educational success. Child athletes would then most likely develop confidence, improve their chances for upward social mobility, and have a better chance of happiness and success throughout life.

Athletes who are in the limelight from early in their careers are labeled as talented individuals. The recognition they attain often leads them to want more attention in the future. Many become more outgoing and interested in gaining prestige both during the school years and later, which may in turn lead to the development of a better self-concept. The result is an individual with stronger beliefs in his or her own abilities. The constant competitive experience in sport often requires that children learn to deal with being compared with others. This evaluation is part of most achievement situations and may help the athlete handle these same pressures in the classroom and increase his or her desire to be a better student. The sport experience also provides athletes with many other skills related to dealing with people, following rules, and leading others.

Holding Your Child Back in School

Recently it has become a more common practice for some parents to force schools to hold their child back to benefit the child's sport performance. This practice has been reported to be common in some areas of the country among parents of eighth-grade boys. These parents want their sons held back so the boys will be bigger and stronger when they enter high school athletics, not because of academic failure. This practice provides an extra year of football eligibility, which may help their child win a scholarship. Although the athletes still only get 4 years of high school eligibility, it allows 19-year-olds to play against 16-, 17-, and 18-year-olds. That's a big year at that age level.

There are many dangers associated with this practice! A student who is retained and does not live up to what is expected can be damaged psychologically. Children kept back for athletic reasons may get bored with school, become disciplinary problems, be hindered in social development, develop sloppy study habits, and accomplish little or nothing academic in that additional year. The extra year can also cut an athlete off from teammates. In addition, the practice is not fair to athletes on other teams who are progressing on schedule.

Qualifying for a Scholarship

In order to qualify for a scholarship to college, your child must be a proven athlete of high quality. If he or she has played well enough in high school or in junior competitions, the chances are he or she will be recruited by some college or university. If not, it still may be possible to go on to college and try out for the team. In fact, many "walk-ons" are able to play the first year and then earn a scholarship by the second year.

There are several advantages to having been a good competitive player before college. In particular, competition provides a proving ground on which your child can match his skills against other similar participants. It also provides an opportunity to develop a reputation against other individuals, which may help your child build confidence as well as provide a "relative" evaluation criteria for a potential coach.

There are at least five essential requirements for high quality skills. These five areas are also the ones that most coaches evaluate before they award a scholarship to a potential student athlete:

- Physical skills—above average talent and physical makeup
- Mental discipline—the ability to concentrate, practice, and be coached
- Goal directedness and emotional stability
- Family support—a willingness to invest resources and provide psychological support and encouragement
- Advice and competition—good coaching and competitive opportunities

A college scholarship may provide excellent sport experience for your child, but it should also lead to a good education along the way. Your child may turn out to be a great professional athlete, but if not, he or she must be capable of finishing that college degree and pursuing a happy and productive adult life.

Deciding Upon an Education

Parents should actively help their child select a college or university. Recruiting, in some cases, borders on outright deceit or insanity. College recruiters can place extreme pressure on young 17-year-old athletes. A parent can provide an outlet for the young athlete's fears and frustrations during the recruiting period, as well as provide encouragement and insight. At this point in life, parents must encourage academic goals to ensure their children do not get caught up in the abuses of the college athletic system.

A university All-American football player, a sure-bet early round pro draft choice as a defensive player, offers this advice to parents and young athletes:

Parents guide their child through many hurts and joys. A main responsibility for parents is to make certain their child emphasizes both academics and athletics. Although it is not obvious to young athletes, an athletic career can end abruptly from injury, being cut, or losing interest.

I know as an athlete in high school I concentrated more on sport, which brought prestige and recognition. My parents quickly brought me to the realization that I had to change my priorities. It happened to me when I was really being noticed by newspapers and colleges. I was a member of the track team in my school and had beaten everyone in the district in the 100-yard dash. I knew I would easily win the regionals, but report cards came out on the day before the meet. To my surprise I received a "D" on my report card, which disturbed me and my parents. I decided I would do something about it during the next 6 weeks. My parents had other plans. I would do something immediately. They decided that instead of going to the track meet, at which I was destined to be the star, I would go home after school and on weekends and study until my grades improved. At the time I thought it was kind of harsh for one poor grade and I didn't realize the logic behind their decision. I began to put more time into studying and now I am getting a good education. It wouldn't have been possible if I had not been made to rearrange my priorities by my parents. Now I really appreciate their decision.

Parents are our guidance counselors. They should help us make decisions that will have a positive effect on our lives. My parents still give me advice, but now I can decide whether to follow it or not. But I always seek out their advice and listen to it before making important decisions.

There are several things my parents did to influence my life as an athlete. Most importantly they taught me to be honest with myself, to accept myself for who and what I am while striving to constantly improve my weaknesses. My parents taught me that being a gifted athlete didn't make me better than others, including my brothers and sisters.

When I was going to make my decision on where to go to college, I asked my parents where I should go and they said it was up to me because it was my future. They said I had to choose and take responsibility for the decision. They did not want me to ever say that it was their fault if my college career didn't work out as planned. Thankfully, I am happy with my choice and don't have any regrets.

There are valid reasons you should be concerned about your child athlete getting a quality education when he or she goes to college, especially if he or she attends a major university on scholarship. Some major universities appear to be much more interested in developing successful athletic teams than in seeing to it that the athletes who make success possible get quality educations. This has been especially true for black athletes.

Dr. Harry Edwards, a leading sport sociologist from the University of California at Berkeley, has written extensively on the topic of black athletes and sport. He suggests in his book, *The Struggle That Must Be* (1980), that parents consider the following:

1. Know the junior high school or high school coaches guiding your child's early athletic development, and know them well! Coaches are not only teaching fundamental skills and techniques; through their words, actions, and attitudes, coaches greatly influence athletes' perspectives on sport and their sense of sports' proper priority in their lives.

2. Parents should thoroughly investigate alternative means of securing financial support at the schools their prospective collegiate athletes are interested in attending. Many times additional support is available beyond the athletic scholarship. Such aid can be secured without affecting opportunities for sport participation.

3. Parents should stipulate in writing to high school coaches that no collegiate athletic recruiter or coach may contact their child without expressed parental consent. This is particularly important since the act of contact can severely limit the amount of support student athletes can receive, regardless of its source.

4. Parents of prospective college athletes should not presume the academic integrity of an athletic department's sport program based upon the academic reputation of the college or university. It must be remembered that in America intercollegiate sports departments have traditionally been regarded as the illegitimate children of the academic community. Evidence suggests that the academic outcomes of scholarship athletes recruited to schools with high academic reputations are not significantly different from those of schools that are less highly regarded academically. The significant consideration is not the academic reputation of the college or university but whether or not the school has developed or is attempting to build a big-time sports program.

5. Parents of prospective intercollegiate athletes should request that the schools in question provide documentation indicating graduation rates for scholarship athletes over the previous 5 years. It may also help to ask about the academic fields of study for the athletes, the average length of time spent in school, any differences between black and white or male and female athletes, and the amount of funds paid directly to tutors. (pp. 237-238)

Information regarding the academic programs of schools should be provided by the administrations of those schools. If there is any hesitation on their part, be sure to check carefully. It is very important that you and your child know the NCAA guidelines and know what to expect from the schools.

Sport and Personal Development

If your child is to have a happy, successful life, he or she must possess good social skills and positive personality traits as well as academic ability. Sport offers opportunities to promote your child's personal growth in these areas.

Enhancing Social Skills

Athletes are generally very sociable individuals. Not only are they friendly, they also know how to act in public and take responsibility for their own actions. Some people may find that hard to believe, but when compared with other individuals of similar backgrounds, athletes are less likely to be deviant in their social behavior. Athletes are less likely to be delinquents than nonathletes from similar areas, possibly because athletes learn to follow rules and are generally more conventional in their life-styles.

Most athletes must learn how to use their time well. They dedicate a great deal of time and energy to their sport and as a result must make good use of their free time. Typically there are rules and sanctions to control an athlete's behavior, even during free time. This will cause many athletes to think twice before failing to conform or behaving in a manner that jeopardizes their athletic careers. Athletes also learn to work toward the overall good of the team. They pride themselves in representing others and contributing to a common goal. These attitudes are not only good for sport but also represent the foundation upon which our society is built.

Building Character

For years, sport administrators have suggested that sport is one of the best avenues available to youngsters for the development of positive personality characteristics. However, in recent years many people have questioned this viewpoint.

Studies have found that athletes possess personality characteristics considered to be important for success in most adult endeavors.

Sport is an achievement situation and reflects values accepted by our society. Therefore, sport may reinforce behavioral qualities important to success in life.

It is difficult to prove that personality characteristics are indeed a result of sport experience. Some scholars who have studied the issue have argued that the sport world merely selects at a very early age those athletes with highly desirable characteristics and eliminates the youngsters who do not have them. This viewpoint may be accurate. However, most adults who have directed sport programs strongly believe that sport participation influences the development of character. There is no clear answer at this time. But let's look closer at some factors that will quite likely affect the amount and kind of character developed in sport.

The most important factor involved in character development through sport probably is the attitude of the coach. Does the coach value hard work and dedication? Does the coach attempt to motivate young athletes who value hard work and dedication? Or does the coach value winning over all else and allow many highly talented but lazy or undisciplined athletes to receive most of the rewards? This latter approach often can have the effect of frustrating many dedicated athletes. Rewarding people who do not work hard will teach the other athletes that unless they are born with talent they are not likely to succeed in sport or work. This is far from the truth!

Effective coaches emphasize the importance of each athlete's developing his or her talent to its fullest. Coaches should stress that anyone can be a success at an appropriately chosen level if he or she wants it badly enough and is willing to work for it. Of course, the best way for these lessons to be learned is through the good example of coaches and parents. These are extremely valuable lessons that can be directly transferred to other areas of life.

Self-discipline and self-control often are assumed to be developed as a result of sport participation. Sport is most assuredly an ideal medium for teaching these values, but when discipline and control are displayed in sport it is often because they have been imposed by a coach. One might question whether or not self-control and self-discipline really have been learned, for in its extreme, the discipline and control in sport may be blind obedience to authority figures, which is less than ideal. Effective coaches will be sure that this is not the case, at least for experienced athletes in their programs.

Coaches, as well as parents, must explain to youngsters the reasons for discipline and control and allow youngsters to discipline and control their own behaviors. When this is done, children learn that they are responsible for their own behavior. In addition, they learn about self-control, probably one of the most important lessons in life.

Many other positive qualities *can* be developed through sport. Self-confidence and sportsmanship can mature in the sport experience. But despite opportunities, athletes will only learn these qualities if coaches and parents believe they are important. These qualities are not guaranteed by-products of sport participation. If they are to be learned as a result of sport, their value should be explained to athletes with judicious use of rewards and attractive models.

Athletics can be an ideal training ground for the development of self-confidence. Confidence is gained not only during actual participation but also through the quality of interactions with teammates and other athletes during sport participation. In addition, fellow students greatly value the friendship and camaraderie of athletes, an experience that can greatly influence the growth of self-confidence.

In conclusion, sport participation can have an extremely beneficial impact on the future success and happiness of your child. The degree to which participation develops positive personality characteristics is dependent upon many things. Most important, however, are the values, attitudes, and behaviors emphasized by your child's coaches and you, the parents.

Summary

Participating in competitive sport can provide many benefits to your child. Athletes often do well academically, and there are many other possible benefits, including the development of achievement motivation, habits of hard work and concentration, and even the attitudes of fair play and honesty. Unfortunately, these are not automatic outcomes of sport participation. They require your intervention and guidance. Be sure to guide your child through the difficult tasks of obtaining a scholarship and choosing a school. The pressure on young athletes who choose to play at the college level can be enormous.

As your child grows, carefully observe his or her development. The temptations to push too hard, overprotect, spoil, or academically delay a child are great. But through careful planning, caring, and communicating, the sport experience can be a very positive one.

Final Questions
and Thoughts

Chapter 15

Parents must make important decisions concerning the happy and successful enrichment of their child in athletics. It may be helpful to consider questions that have been asked by other parents, because their experiences may help you make decisions about your child. These questions then will be followed by some final thoughts about being a parent, including a code of ethics for parents.

Parents' Questions

Question: Is it normal for a young athlete to sulk after a loss? If not, what should I do about it?

Answer: Most children will not sulk for an extended period of time. However, it is normal for them to be disappointed and discouraged for a short period of time, perhaps an hour or so. This period of disappointment can last even longer if the loss was in a particularly important contest or was a surprising defeat coupled with a poor performance.

If your child is sulking for a long time, days or weeks, you must be concerned. Have a serious talk with him or her. First, make certain the child isn't sulking just to show you and others how much he or she cares. Parents sometimes unintentionally teach sulking behavior as an ineffective way to show commitment. However, once you are sure that there is a real concern or disappointment, help your child to realize such a response will surely lead to more failure. Sulking will flood the young athlete's mind and body with negative thoughts and feelings. These in turn may produce sleepless nights, affect concentration, interfere with eating habits, and isolate the child from teammates, friends, and coaches.

When your child sulks for a short time following a discouraging performance, don't be concerned and don't force your child to talk about it. Wait until he or she is ready. When your child is ready to talk, be a good listener. Accept the fact that for the moment your child's dreams are shattered. Gradually help him or her to evaluate the performance honestly and accurately and focus on how enjoyable it will be when success does come. This is a good way to renew your child's interest in getting back to practice.

Question: My child has been doing very well in sport, but is never happy. She never seems satisfied no matter how well she performs. How can I help her?

Answer: Your child may tend to be a perfectionist, which may be good in motivating her but may work against her. There is a fine line between a perfectionistic tendency that can help a young athlete develop her potential to the fullest and the possibility that perfectionism will become an obsession and stand in her way.

Help your child realize the importance of cherishing success, because successful moments have great potential for energizing your child for future progress. To negate such an opportunity is self-defeating.

Your child must realize that even the greats she watches on television took time to develop their skills. They also had ups and downs when they were young athletes. Like them, your child must learn to redefine success and enjoy the struggles of "getting there."

Your child needs to learn to enjoy the present and wait a day or two before considering how to improve. Focusing on the past or preparing for the future should not get in the way of enjoying the present.

Question: My child is achieving success as a young athlete but has been quite discouraged lately because he doesn't seem to have any friends. The harder he tries to gain some, the more isolated he feels. How can I help him help himself?

Answer: This is a problem that many young athletes experience, particularly those who feel they must prove their worth to others through their performance. Often such athletes aren't really sure of themselves. Perhaps they do not like themselves. As a result they boast about themselves and put others down. Soon others recognize that such athletes are insecure and choose not to fraternize with them.

Your child must realize that people like people who like themselves, because such individuals are happy and display enthusiasm and optimism. They exude self-confidence through their actions rather than their words and do not make fun of others. Other children will like your child if he knows how to be a good listener and responds to the needs and interests of his friends.

A good way to begin to help your child cultivate the skill of earning friends is to ask him to make a list of three people he would like to have as friends and three he would not like to have as friends. Then ask him to list five to seven qualities in each of these individuals. Finally, have him study these lists for positive qualities he might try to adopt and negative qualities he should reject or avoid. This exercise may help him discover his best attributes.

Question: What can I do to help my child like herself more? She is constantly putting herself down.

Answer: There are lots of young athletes with this tendency. Despite being healthy and coordinated, they do not seem to like themselves. They constantly engage in self-ridicule: They do not like their builds; they think they are ugly; they believe they are not as quick as a teammate; or they criticize aloud every mistake they make.

First, your child must learn the art of self-encouragement. Sport is difficult enough without the added burden of private and public self-criticism. Your child will gain nothing by criticizing aspects of herself that cannot be changed. Many young athletes who are highly motivated develop a tendency to criticize themselves because they constantly compare themselves to athletes who are slightly better. They get lost in self-criticism when their time would be much better spent focusing on steps toward improvement.

Nothing beneficial ever results from frequent self-criticism. As Eleanor Roosevelt once said, "No one can make you dislike yourself but you." Your child must learn this.

As a parent, you must ask yourself what kind of model you have provided for your child. Are you a perfectionist? Has your child learned from you? If so, don't despair. The good news is your child loves, respects, and is imitating you, so you can change your actions and those of your child.

Your child must learn from your example to love herself. She does not have to publicly broadcast her self-love to the point of being conceited. To do so could isolate her from others. But your child must realize that it is important for her to like herself. She should be able to look into the mirror each morning and say, "I like me." She should be happy because she is trying regardless of whether she wins or loses. Equating happiness and self-acceptance with performance results is both irrational and self-defeating. Sport is only one part of your child's life. It is appropriate for her to be disappointed with her play or results, but she still must like herself. She still is a worthy person.

You might also like to try the "poker chip trick." Ask your child to make a list of her positive and negative qualities. Put a chip in a "good" pile for each positive quality and a different colored chip in the "not-so-good" pile. She will probably be pleasantly surprised at how much larger the "good" pile is.

Question: Are there any ways to help my child learn to think positive thoughts about himself? Can I help him build self-confidence?

Answer: As previously mentioned, your child needs to learn how to talk to himself in a positive, self-enhancing manner. Teach him the "thought stoppage" technique of telling himself "stop" each time he has a negative thought about himself. Then have him replace the negative thought with a positive statement. For example, if he is telling himself that he is never going to hit this pitcher's fast ball, he should say: "STOP. I have been practicing against fast balls all week and if I concentrate, I will do well." Although it is often said that positive thinking is both powerful and influential, it is less frequently mentioned that negative thinking is just as powerful and influential—in the opposite direction. Negative thinking drains rather than provides energy.

Self-confidence will not suddenly appear overnight. Some young athletes feel that they won't start competing or practicing diligently until they become self-confident, but this type of thinking is backwards. Self-confidence grows out of being willing to practice carefully and then taking the risk to compete. It comes from feeling good about past successes and the efforts expended to reach those successes.

Your child's attitude toward life in general and sport in particular is critical. Your child must be willing to set goals and work toward them during competition despite the fact that there is no guarantee of success. Your child should view obstacles as exciting challenges and good experiences. Competition is the place to learn and to improve. If your child holds this attitude, he will view defeats and obstacles as momentary and they will not immobilize him. Therefore, it is crucial to get your child to participate in a sport on a regular basis. The more he persists, the more success he will experience and the more confidence he will develop.

Your job as a parent is to provide support and encouragement during the rough moments and the frustrations that are sure to occur. This support will help your child realize he can control his own destiny and be confident he will get what he desires.

Question: What should I say to my child right before she plays someone whom she has never played before?

Answer: Begin by reminding your child that situations such as this are a major part of the excitement of sport. She should desire rather than fear the unknown or unfamiliar. You must help your child learn the advantage of going into such a contest with the attitude "I am better than you until proven otherwise," which is a much more positive attitude than "You are better than I am until I prove otherwise." The latter approach usually leads to failure, and an athlete never knows if she lost because she wasn't as good as the opponent or because she didn't believe in herself. As a result, little positive gain occurs. The self-defeating approach also causes her to focus on her opponent, whom she cannot control, instead of herself.

Help your child to realize that she will enjoy playing against an unfamiliar team or opponent. This is the real challenge of sport, and a quality that will allow her to be different from most people. Too many athletes who never reach their potential are so comfortable with what is familiar that they will never risk failure by competing in unfamiliar situations.

The development of this positive attitude will also allow your child to try new skills, strategies, techniques, and training methods without fear. You want your child to enjoy trying new ideas, because rejecting potentially useful ideas without trying them is self-defeating.

Let's face it, if your young athlete is intimidated by the unknown or the unfamiliar, she will have difficulties in sport. Your child needs to learn to enjoy actively seeking out the unknown. She will definitely benefit from "going for it!"

Question: My child gets really uptight when I come to watch him during competition. Is there anything I can do to help?

Answer: First, ask your child if he realizes how uptight he is. If he does, ask what he thinks is causing the problem. It may be your mere presence or his concern that you will be embarrassed. Maybe he doesn't want you to attend his contests for a while. He may wish to have you move away from the field of play when you do attend. Perhaps he is trying too hard to please you and thinks you will only love him if he wins. Take the time to talk with your child about these issues. Let him know that in your mind he is a winner regardless of how he plays. It may help a great deal.

Your child, however, may be putting pressure on himself. He needs to learn to compete for himself rather than for others. He has probably not yet learned how to manage his nervousness.

You may begin to help your child by putting sport into its proper perspective, because he probably thinks sport is more important than it really is. Remind him that sport success as measured by wins and losses will not guarantee health, happiness, or personal satisfaction. After all, how important is it to put a ball through a hoop, into a goal, between two posts, over a net, over a fence, or into a hole? It is the process and enjoyment of trying to learn how to do so consistently that gives sport its true meaning.

Question: I have often heard it said that athletes must be committed. What does this really mean?

Answer: Being committed means your child knows what she wants and is willing to work diligently to attain it. It means your child has the self-discipline to sacrifice some immediate pleasures for the long-term pleasure of accomplishing her goal. It means she is willing to persist when others quit, to make sport an integral part of her life.

A highly successful athlete, Martina Navratilova, told a story about being committed. She said she used to be "involved" in tennis and in 1982 decided to be "committed." She joked about the difference being similar to the disparity between the pig and the chicken in ham and eggs. The chicken is involved, the pig is totally committed!

Question: How can I help my child to be goal oriented and committed? Can a young athlete be successful and still enjoy living every day of his life?

Answer: It is important for your child to realize that while goals are important to success and happiness, they can also stand in the way. Goals can become more important than living in the present and enjoying each day.

Certainly an athlete must be dedicated enough to stick to his goals. This may involve certain sacrifices. But he must also be adaptable enough to adjust his goals when an unplanned, desirable experience comes along. Of course, if such experiences occur every day, he will not achieve his goals. So your child must have goals, enjoy striving for them, and yet not allow them to control his life to the point of never enjoying the present.

The question suggests that perhaps you should ask your child what he enjoys. Being goal oriented will be easiest if he is committed to goals he wants and enjoys.

Question: My child is 12 years old and has been a gymnast for the past 6 years. She seems to have lost interest. Could she possibly be burned out at this young age?

Answer: It certainly is possible. This problem is surfacing quite frequently today with young athletes. The rigors of constant training and the pressures of performance combined with adult supervision have the potential for taking the fun out of sport. Suddenly what once was fun becomes drudgery.

A young athlete who is burned out will begin to question her commitment to sport, feel discouraged, and lack energy for concentrated practice and performance. With time, a negative attitude toward the sport develops.

For many youngsters, the cure is a 1-week to 3-month break from practice and competition to allow the worn-out mind and body to heal. Some young athletes may actually need to quit their sport and try another. Others simply need to find a coach who can keep the fun in practice.

A number of young athletes have overcome this difficulty by simply shortening their practice periods for a while. It may also help to limit the frequency of competition and adjust your child's level of commitment. Potential burnout candidates often find they have become so committed to sport that they don't enjoy any other experiences in life. These athletes simply need to reorganize their time and their schedules to meet new priorities. The happiness of enjoying friends, a night out, a day spent relaxing, or a family vacation can cause an almost immediate improvement in performance and enthusiasm. A mini-vacation can renew the excitement of their sport.

The worst thing you can do is to get mad at the child for being burned out and remind her of the money you have spent and the hours you have invested. The pressure and guilt will only add to the problem. Sol Gordon in *The Teenage Survival Book* (1981) recently identified 15 phrases that were guaranteed to turn off or "flame up" your child:

1. I want to have a serious talk with you . . .
2. We trust you . . .
3. When I was your age . . .
4. Because we say so!
5. As long as I don't know about it . . .
6. Act your age!
7. It's about time!
8. Ask your father (or mother) . . .
9. Are you telling me the truth?
10. That's not your idea, is it?
11. Don't you dare talk to me that way!
12. Get off your high horse . . .
13. Wipe that smile off your face!
14. After all we've done for you . . .   (p. 81)

Such statements only add to your child's guilt or concern about being burned out. Instead, try to find the reason for this mental and physical fatigue and help her overcome it.

Question: Is there ever a time when you should tell your child his goals are too high? Should you help him understand that they may be unrealistic and suggest he should lower his expectations or switch sports?

Answer: Most definitely! Unfortunately, though, this is one of the most difficult decisions you will make because it is almost impossible to be certain that goals are unrealistic. This is why most great accomplishments begin with dreams and require short-term and intermediate goals.

But there are situations where a parent, with the advice of a knowledgeable coach or physical educator, can and should let a young athlete know his goals are unrealistic.

These decisions are easiest to make in situations where physical or genetic traits are most important to top level performance. For example, in short sprint events in track and swimming all the diligent practice in the world will not allow an athlete without the appropriate genetic endowment to be competitive with others so blessed. The same may be true for athletes with large frames in a sport such as gymnastics or for small players in football, volleyball, or basketball.

You must realize, however, that exceptions are always possible. Small players do become successful in "big men" sports, but not very often. The important point is that once you have talked to your child, it is his decision. Can he be happy competing with himself, perhaps performing to his fullest potential, and still not experiencing success relative to others? This may be a reality with which your child may need to come to grips, because if he doesn't, he may become frustrated and turned off by sport. The result is often an athlete who thinks sport is not fair because he has not achieved success despite persistent effort whereas others did with little effort. Then you will have to tell him he is right! Life isn't always fair. Success does not always come to those who work the hardest.

Question: Gosh, these problems sound so minor. My child is 12 years old and has no interest in sport. He never wants to do anything. When I ask him, "What would you like to do?" he says something like "I don't know," "It doesn't make any difference," "What do you want to do?" or "There's nothing to do." How can I help motivate him?

Answer: This is indeed a perplexing problem. You must begin by being an excited and enthusiastic model yourself. If you have been a good model and still feel your child has acted negatively, you may need to back off and not let your child know how much you care.

The other possibility is to take your child up on his offer: "What do you want to do?" Select an activity and do it with him on a regular basis. It is amazing how many children who seem uninterested and bored simply have a lack of confidence. If you will spend enough time with him so his skill level can develop, his confidence will grow, as will the corresponding interest and enthusiasm. It often helps to practice or play with such young athletes in an isolated environment because they may find it hard to perform in front of others if they are not yet skilled. After they develop some confidence in their skills, they will be ready to perform publicly.

Despite the best of attempts by parents, however, sometimes a child just won't like sport. If that happens, leave the child alone. Some day he might get interested. If not, at least he'll be happy and still enjoy his parents and himself.

Watching Your Child Grow

Watching your child grow will be a major source of pleasure for you. You'll be able to look back on and enjoy the excitement of being a parent, and you will have many wonderful memories. During pregnancy, like all parents, you begin to fantasize. "What will our child become?" "I sure hope he or she will be happy, healthy, and coordinated." You discuss your expectations and have exciting dreams about your child, dreams that undoubtedly influence what your child will become. After birth, you become attached to your child. The novelty is exciting. But with time, you begin to wonder what effect the child will have upon your freedom. You may even periodically search for identity and meaning in your life. You develop a need to find time for both the baby and yourself.

The desire to raise your child in the best way possible is ever present. You provide love. You're happy and warm in front of the baby. You exercise the baby and give him or her the right food. Balls, bats, and various other kinds of sport equipment dominate the baby's room.

At this point, parents tend to become increasingly interested in how to raise the perfect child or be the perfect parent. You may find it helpful to consider a general model of behavior related to sport. Such a model is presented in the code of ethics for parents.

Code of Ethics for Parents

1. I will help my child learn to enjoy sport and develop the skills that he or she is capable of performing.
2. I will learn the strengths and weaknesses of my child so that I might place the young athlete into situations where he or she has a maximum opportunity for success.
3. I will become thoroughly familiar with the techniques and rules of the sport my child chooses.

4. I will do my best to learn the fundamental teaching skills and strategies related to my child's sport.
5. I will practice and help my child so that he or she will have an opportunity for skill improvement through active participation.
6. I will communicate with my child the rights and responsibilities of others who are involved in sport.
7. I will protect the health and safety of my child by insisting that all of the activities under my control are conducted for his or her psychological and physiological welfare.
8. I will treat each player, opposing coach, official, parent, and administrator with respect and dignity.
9. I will uphold the authority of officials and coaches who are working with my child. I will assist them when possible and use good judgment if I disagree with them.
10. I will become familiar with the objectives of the sport programs with which my child is affiliated.
11. I will strive to help select activities that uphold our family values.
12. I will help my child develop good sportsmanship and a desire to strive for success.

This code of ethics will be a great help to some parents. Others may decide, "Heck, we're the experts. It's our child. Let's just be ourselves and do our best. Let's relax and enjoy raising our child. Let's face it, every child is different so no one can really tell us how to raise our child."

The enthusiasm of most parents intensifies as the child approaches the preschool years. "She looks just like me." "He's a chip off the old block." "Gosh, do you believe how coordinated she is? She's smoother than I am already. Thank goodness!" "Let's make sure we give our child the opportunities we didn't have." "I think he is going to be a star!"

These feelings and beliefs about your child may continue, and your child may indeed grow to be a star. But most parents slowly realize that although their child may be special, he or she is neither perfect nor a superstar. Don't expect too much, but be realistic and supportive as you provide the best possible experiences for your child.

As your child passes through the elementary school years, many exciting experiences occur that you will never forget. Your child runs faster, throws farther, and catches a ball better. He or she smiles with pride at your enjoyment. When your friends come to visit, your child shows them his or her new moves—the forward roll, the handstand, the dive into the pool, the soccer kick.

Later you will recall the first time your child tried out for a team, the day your child came home with a uniform, the nights your child slept with a new racket or glove, or that first trophy. How happy and content your child was! The world seemed simple. You will remember your child's excitement about an upcoming game and how he or she begged you to go to the game and watch. When your child entered the game, he or she looked at you and waved. After the game, your child bragged, regardless of his or her performance.

Your child will go through moments of discouragement and great joy. You'll never forget how sad your child was after failing, or how happy your child was after succeeding and how pleased you were! You'll remember how later, after your child went to bed, you talked about the joys of parenthood, how you wished you could make every day a successful one for him or her. You'll never forget those days and nights.

Your child advances through high school and college. Maybe he or she becomes a star and earns a scholarship—maybe not. Either way, you have learned to keep your child's sport experience in perspective. You know in retrospect that you are glad that you and your child gave sport a chance, because you shared many great moments together as a result. Your child learned how to compete, how to enjoy winning, how to respond to failure, and how to improve.

Sport has been a great experience for you and your child. You know now that winning isn't everything. No one always wins. But through sport your child made many friends and learned to like and appreciate his or her mind and body. Because of sport, your child learned to value a good education. You know now that your child had a chance to learn a lifelong attitude of hard work that can lead to happiness and success. You have done a great job!

References

Brooks, L.D. (1976, September 2). Letter to my football coach. *The Leaguer*, p. 2.

Browing, G. (1980, December). The figure of a swimmer. *Swimmers Magazine*, p. 50.

Close, B. (1978, December). The real meaning of winning. *Swimmers Magazine*, p. 12.

Coulson, R.H. (1978, December). He comes in second. *Swimmers Magazine*, p. 12.

Dennis, L. (1982, January). Kite. *Golf Digest*, p. 30.

Edwards, H. (1980). *The struggle that must be*. New York: MacMillan.

Fisher, C. (1982, June). *Do's and don'ts for self-confidence*. Paper presented at the annual Sport Psychology Conference, Charlottesville, VA.

Garrity, J. (1981, August 17). Love and hate in El Segundo. *Sports Illustrated*, pp. 52-56, 58-61, 63-64, 66.

Gordon, S. (1981). *The teenage survival book*. New York: The New York Times Book Company.

Jackson, R. (1981, November 30). Two born winners. *Sports Illustrated*, pp. 82, 85.

Lopez, N. (1981, May). Tips to parents of junior players. *Golf Digest*, p. 136.

Love, D. (1982, January). Finding the right teacher for your child. *Golf Digest*, p. 20.

Moore, K. (1981, May 11). The three-sport man: Hail and farewell. *Sports Illustrated*, pp. 66-70, 72, 74, 77, 80.

Newman, B. (1981, January 19). The master of disaster. *Sports Illustrated*, pp. 32-35.

Newman, B. (1981, December 5). Rookies on tour. *Sky*, pp. 5-13.

Power, T. (1980, June-July). Can the Caulkins sisters survive success? *Swimmers Magazine*, p. 6.

Schultz, D. (1981, December 11). Inside track. *Inside Sport*, pp. 11-15.

Stuart, J. (1978, December). How to survive the car pool. *Swimmers Magazine*, p. 9.

Telander, R. (1982, August 30). Paving the way for $$$. *Sports Illustrated*, pp. 38-39, 42-45.

Thomas, J.R. (Ed.). (1980). *Youth sports guide for coaches and parents*. Washington, DC: AAHPERD Publications.

Underwood, J. (1981, December 14). Catch a catching star. *Sports Illustrated*, pp. 34-38, 40.

Wheeler, E. (1980, November). Juvenile court: The Andrea Jaeger decision. *Women's Sports*, pp. 26-29.

Whicker, M. (1982, September). You can't get Pittsburgh out of the boy. *Inside Sports*, pp. 56-57.

Zimbardo, P.G., & Radl, S.L. (1981). *The shy child*. New York: McGraw-Hill.

Suggested Readings

Braden, V., & Bruns, B. (1980). *Teaching children tennis the Vic Braden way.* Boston: Little, Brown.

Bunker, L.K., Johnson, C.E., & Parker, J.E. (1983). *Motivating kids through play.* New York: Leisure Press.

Coakley, J.J. (1978). *Sports in society: Issues and controversies.* St. Louis: C.V. Mosby.

Edwards, H. (1980). *The struggle that must be.* New York: MacMillan.

Feltz, D.L., & Weiss, M.R. (1982). Developing self-efficacy through sport. *Journal of Physical Education, Recreation, and Dance,* **53**, 24-26.

Harris, D.V., & Harris, B.L. (1984). *The athlete's guide to sports psychology: Mental skills for physical people.* New York: Leisure Press.

Lange, A., & Jakubowski, P. (1976). *Responsible assertive behavior: Cognitive/behavioral procedures for trainers.* Champaign, IL: Research Press.

Loehr, J. (1982). *Athletic excellence: Mental toughness training for sports.* Denver: Forum.

Martens, R. (1978). *Joy and sadness in children's sports.* Champaign, IL: Human Kinetics.

Martinek, T.J., Crowe, P.B., & Rejeski, W.J. (1982). *Pygmalion in the gym: Causes and effects of expectations in teaching and coaching.* West Point, NY: Leisure Press.

Orlick, T. (1980). *In pursuit of excellence.* Champaign, IL: Human Kinetics.

Orlick, T., & Botterill, C. (1980). *Every kid can win*. Chicago: Nelson-Hall.

Pate, R., McClanahan, B., & Rotella, R.J. (1984). *Scientific foundations of coaching*. Philadelphia: W.B. Saunders.

Index

About the Authors

Currently the director of the sport psychology program at the University of Virginia, Robert Rotella has spent many years teaching and directing sport programs for children and young adults. He has taught physical education at schools for the athletically gifted and for the mentally retarded, and has coached high school and college athletes, as well as athletes in the Special Olympics. Dr. Rotella presently serves as a sport psychology consultant to many Olympic and professional athletes, college athletes from the University of Virginia, and developing young athletes. He earned his PhD from the University of Connecticut in 1976. As an undergraduate, Dr. Rotella was a Club Lacrosse All-American and a participant in the North-South All-Star game. He was twice named in Outstanding College Athletes of America.

Linda Bunker, director of the Motor Learning Laboratory at the University of Virginia, was a varsity athlete in tennis, field hockey, and basketball at the University of Illinois, where she earned her PhD in 1973. She has taught both elementary and secondary physical education and is a consultant for the National Golf Foundation. She also has coached both young athletes and college athletes, from recreational sport participants to young professional golf and tennis players. Dr. Bunker has served on the Youth Sports Task Force of the National Association of Sport and Physical Education, where she helped to develop guidelines for youth sport participation. She is presently on the advisory board for the Women's Sports Foundation, and also works as a consultant to amateur and professional athletes.

Robert Rotella and Linda Bunker have coauthored several other books, including *Mind Mastery for Winning Golf; Mind, Set, and Match for Winning Tennis,* and *Sport Psychology: Maximizing Sport Performance.* Both were contributing authors to the *Youth Sport Guide for Parents and Coaches.* Dr. Bunker also wrote *Motivating Kids Through Play* and *Golf: Better Practice for Better Play* (with De De Owens), both published by Leisure Press.